MARK TWAIN
Strange & Wonderful

Lee Prosser

With Debra Prosser

Schiffer Publishing Ltd®

4880 Lower Valley Road, Atglen, Pennsylvania 19310

Schiffer Books are available at special discounts for bulk purchases for sales promotions or premiums. Special editions, including personalized covers, corporate imprints, and excerpts can be created in large quantities for special needs. For more information contact the publisher:

Published by Schiffer Publishing Ltd.
4880 Lower Valley Road
Atglen, PA 19310
Phone: (610) 593-1777; Fax: (610) 593-2002
E-mail: Info@schifferbooks.com

For the largest selection of fine reference books on this and related subjects,
please visit our website at: **www.schifferbooks.com**
We are always looking for people to write books on new and related subjects.
If you have an idea for a book, please contact us at **proposals@schifferbooks.com**

This book may be purchased from the publisher.
Include $5.00 for shipping.
Please try your bookstore first.
You may write for a free catalog.

In Europe, Schiffer books are distributed by
Bushwood Books
6 Marksbury Ave.
Kew Gardens
Surrey TW9 4JF England
Phone: 44 (0) 20 8392 8585; Fax: 44 (0) 20 8392 9876
E-mail: info@bushwoodbooks.co.uk
Website: www.bushwoodbooks.co.uk

Other Schiffer Books by the Author:
Branson Hauntings, 978-0-7643-3402-3, $14.99
Midwest Hauntings, 978-0-7643-3605-8, $14.99
Missouri Hauntings, 978-0-7643-3119-0, $14.99
UFOs in Missouri: True Tales of Extraterrestrials and Related Phonomena, 978-0-7643-3747-5, $16.99

Designed by Mark David Bowyer
Type set in EngraversRoman Bd BT / NewBaskerville BT

ISBN: 978-0-7643-3881-6
Printed in the United States of America

CONTENTS

Acknowledgments
& Dedication

Special thanks to Mark Twain, who made it possible with his massive outpouring of writings and speeches, and to the public and school libraries who keep his books in demand and available, and to the worldwide readers who continue to make Mark Twain one of their favorite authors. Thank you, too, for the Internet, which has over ten million sites about aspects of Mark Twain's life available to readers worldwide.

Many thanks to my wonderful editors, Dinah Roseberry and Jennifer Marie Savage, for without their help and encouragement this book would not have been written.

Special thanks to my wife, Debra, my daughters Dawn and Mandy; my grandchildren Makela, Malakai, and Katy; and my step-daughter Elizabeth and her son Johnathan.

A Note from the Author's Family

*L*ee Prosser was and has been many things in this lifetime. The one thing that was most important to him was his study of the teaching of Vedanta. It is with this in mind that the following verse has been chosen as something we all agree that best states Lee's beliefs:

'Never was there a time when I did not exist, Nor you, Nor all these Kings: Nor in the future shall any of us cease to be.' ~~ Bhagavad-gita 2.12.

Sadly, Lee passed away before this book's publication. This is an original work of nonfiction about one of America's most prolific, insightful, satiric, humorous, controversial, and most written about authors. Based on decades of reading and personal research, it is Lee Prosser's interpretation of Mark Twain.

Lee started reading Twain's writings as a six-year-old child. Mark Twain is "America's Man For All Seasons." What he created in fiction and nonfiction will endure as long as people read, and wish to learn from, his insights. Lee proudly dedicates this book to the endearing legend/memory of what, who, and why Mark Twain was and what he achieved during his lifetime as an American writer.

For those interested in what and who Mark Twain was, read what Twain had to say in his numerous letters, speeches, lectures, and stories. Read what Twain's contemporaries had to say about him. This retrospective look of Twain's life only touches the tip. There is a vast amount of information available on Mark Twain in one form or another and worth your time to come to know and understand. We hope that Lee's intriguing interpretation of Twain the man and Twain the writer makes you, his readers, want to discover in more detail the life and legacy of one of our country's greatest writers.

PREFACE

A man sits in a chair, staring out across the swiftly flowing water on a crisp, warm spring day, which is creeping towards sunset, a time when shadows start their play across the water and the riverbanks. There is a thoughtful expression on the man's face as he carefully studies the deep water and quiet riverbanks. He stares and listens for something — some *thing* he senses is there, but has not come into view just yet!

The man leans forward, a smile mixed with respect and curiosity on his face, as the sounds of the river reach out to him. What strange sound does he hear? Is something lurking near the waterline close to where he sits, some strange unseen monster? Is it a ghostly apparition seeking contact...or is it a figment of the Missouri landscape? The man listens intently... *What does he hear?* What runs through his imagination as he listens to the sounds of the mighty river? What does he sense below its dark, fast-flowing current from the safety of his chair on the steamboat deck? What strange things might lurk below?

What is it that Mark Twain is listening to, or is he listening *for* something? What does the Mississippi River whisper in his ears, what secrets are shared with him? What premonition does he feel coming into his mind, what does he sense, and what is his intuition suggesting to him?

Vintage photo of Mark Twain on a steamboat.

Introduction

MARK TWAIN, THE EXISTENTIALIST & HIS MISSISSIPPI RIVER METAPHOR

"The Mississippi is well worth reading about. It is not a commonplace river, but on the contrary is in all ways remarkable."

~ *Life on the Mississippi*, 1883

*I*n looking at Mark Twain's life, it is important to see not only the influence the Mississippi River had on him, but also *how* that Old Man River affected him. To examine an old theme, going back to the Ancient Greeks, "to endure is everything and anything else is secondary," which is precisely how it is explained existentially in contemporary terms. Twain spent some of his early years on the river and encountered the enduring flow of water on a daily basis. The idea that you cannot step twice into the same place in flowing water, or anywhere for that fact, goes back to the Ancient Greek philosopher, Heraclitus of Ephesus (535–475 BCE). The theme of the enduring river registered on Twain as he witnessed it, listened to its dark whispers, and observed it. This became internalized in Twain's mind and in the truest sense of living a meaningful life, as Twain realized that "to endure was everything and anything else was secondary."

To create meaning out of chaos echoes throughout the writings of Mark Twain in the truest sense of existential definition, and his choices were made accordingly, shaping his individual, personal destiny. Twain lived his life in a manner that created meaning out of chaos, and he did it by his own personal choice and inclinations.

This original charcoal drawing of Mark Twain, by internationally-respected English Artist, Terence Kelly, was drawn in October 2010. *From the author's personal art collection.*

Examine *The Adventures of Tom Sawyer* or *The Adventures of Huckleberry Finn* and his famous raft sequence, the story of *Joan of Arc, Pudd'nhead Wilson*, the short fiction, and the later fiction after the loss of loved ones in Twain's life. You can see the themes of endurance and intent focused fully and reflected in the mind of this great American author. To endure is one thing, and to have the intent to endure and go on, is another, and together they are soulmates. This is the true heart, soul, and intellect of the themes found in Mark Twain's writings: endurance and intent.

As a native Missourian, born, reared, and having spent my formative years in the state of Missouri, I, too, have discovered from life's experiences that two themes dominate — endurance and intent — interlocked together in a lasting strength, and anything else is secondary. Mark Twain's legacy for the world endures as a splendid example of a master storyteller, a humorist, an essayist, a novelist, and a speech-maker.

Although there are over four hundred Biblical illusions and references in his writings, it was Thomas Paine's *The Age of Reason* that helped Twain develop a perceptive skepticism towards the Holy Bible and its claims of miracles, leading also to Twain further questioning the justice of a Christian God. He saw violence and danger in the United States, and he observed and understood the American fondness and fascination for such, including blood sports. This in turn led to another enduring theme in Twain's writings — the metaphor of night and the dark.

Twain witnessed many terrifying things as a child and youth and, as a result, was exposed to death at an early age. By 1853, Hannibal, Missouri, had left its indelible mark on Twain. With the death of his attorney-local judge father from pneumonia complications, Twain's childhood came to an end, though it would continue to influenced him throughout his writings and, indeed, his life.

The American psyche is indeed encoded and permanently etched in Mark Twain's writings, which reflect the essence of what it is to be an American. Mark Twain is one of the most important of all United States authors and will remain so, as he introduced colloquial speech into the American language and an existential perspective. He also used insightful imagery in his scenes that brought an added depth to his stories. His perceptive, vivid writings are his legacy to all Americans and for the world.

Two other great American writers and Nobel Prize Literature authors have commented on the enduring greatness of Mark Twain: Ernest Hemingway and William Faulkner. Hemingway stated in his nonfiction book, *The Green Hills of Africa*: "All modern American literature comes from one book by Mark Twain called *Huckleberry Finn*." Faulkner, a contemporary of Hemingway, called Twain "The Father of American literature."

However, it cannot be denied that an interesting, poignant aspect of Mark Twain's life was that the Mississippi River was always with him. Mark Twain would cross many bridges in his life, but it would forever always be the same river for him to cross, wherever he was.

Author's Note: For the reader wishing to learn about the Mississippi River and its history, a good starting place is the well-written and entertaining nonfiction book, The Mississippi River, by Tom Weil. This 514-page book gives an excellent, concise analysis of the culture, nature, and travel sites along the Mississippi River. Through Twain's notebook writings, it becomes clear how the Mississippi River -- and Hannibal's close location to it -- left an everlasting impact on Mark Twain's psyche and his life. In 1904, Twain wrote in his notebook, "The skin of every human being contains a slave."

Having seen the mighty Mississippi River in my lifetime, it is easy to see how this affectionately nicknamed Old Man River held such an influence for Twain and how it permanently marked him for life. There is a serene feel to the water flowing by, but underneath always lurks that hidden psychological undercurrent of darkness and death, for under the serenity of the surface lies the treachery of the watery depths below, a place where death walks awake, and undisturbed in the form of the many ghosts that make their homes there and patiently await future victims! The Mississippi River is America's storehouse for ghosts. There are countless numbers of ghost stories and hauntings that have survived along -- and in -- the river.

Chapter One:

THE EARLY YEARS

"I awoke, and found myself lying with my head out of the bed and 'sagging' downward considerably – a position favorable to dreaming dreams with morals in them, but not poetry."

~ "The Curious Dream," 1870

ark Twain was born November 30, 1835, as Samuel Langhorne Clemens, at Florida, Missouri. He grew up in a very rough rural setting, yet there did exist a tolerant understanding between the black slaves and the white owners in the area. As a growing boy, with pale features and red hair, he would over the period of his childhood be exposed to slave stories of spells, incantations, the magic of the old ways of the slaves, a foreboding sense of retribution, the chanting and singing heard frequently, and scary stories of the walking dead. Much has been written about Mark Twain's attitude toward "Negroes." With the passage of over a century and studies of his correspondence, speeches, nonfiction, and fiction, it has become evident he was ahead of his time in promoting good race-ethnic relations. In 1904, he wrote in his notebook, "The skin of every human being contains a slave."

The Move to Missouri

In November 1839, the entire Clemens family made the move to Hannibal. A slave girl named Jennie went with them. John Marshall Clemens and his wife Jane relocated their large brood to a better setting. Twain's brothers and sisters were Orion Clemens (7/17/1825–12/1/1897), Henry Clemens (7/13/1838–06/21/1858), Pamela Clemens (9/19/1827–8/31/1904), Margaret Clemens (5/31/1830–8/17/1839), Benjamin Clemens (6/08/1832–5/12/1842), and Pleasant Clemens (1828–1829, actual dates unknown).

Twain had an active youth, experiencing all of the joys, hopes, fears, experiments, sadness, disillusions, successes, pleasures, and attributes that would help form his developing attitudes towards living a meaningful life. He had a love for life that was full of vigor and curiosity, and he wanted to know what made life so full of surprises. A shrewd observer of people and human nature, he watched — as well as partook of — what life had to offer, oftentimes with surprising results!

Vintage photo of Mark Twain at age 15.

The themes found in Mark Twain's writings throughout his life reflect situations, encounters, and personal summations he encountered as a youth and a young man. As a youth, Twain developed his early, budding skills of reading people and situations for what they actually were rather than what they appeared to be. He was able to sense intuitively when something seemed awry, and then, if need be at the time, examine that something deeper for the reasons. Twain looked beneath the surface and, over a period of time, his insights and observations became stunning comments on the human condition. In a letter to William T. Stead dated January 9, 1899, Twain wrote: "*Peace by compulsion. That seems a better idea than the other. Peace by persuasion has a pleasant sound, but I think we should not be able to work it. We should have to tame the human race first, and history seems to show that that cannot be done.*"

As mentioned previously, Twain's growing up years contained joys, conflicts, curiosity, imagination, fears, love, happiness, and situations that were his own and reflected not only the time he grew up in, but also the people he grew up with and was around. These were the things that influenced him and colored his attitudes towards life and people.

Twain came to know the black and white approaches of life in the sense he knew from observation that many people simply reacted one way or another and saw things in only one way. Yet, he also came to realize that life was *not* a black and white situation and that there were not only exceptions, but also there was oftentimes a gray area between the black and white approaches that held hidden truths. There were other possibilities to consider and other avenues of interpretation that were honest and valid...and Mark Twain found these other possibilities and avenues. This can be seen in his growing appreciation at seeing the humor in life and the situations each person faces, including him! Not all situations are terrible, not all situations are bad. Simply put, life situations are what you make of them. Even in darkness there is some hope of light.

Twain and the Paranormal

In his younger years, Twain developed an ongoing interest in ghosts, premonitions, and things of a paranormal nature. He also suffered from nightmares, played in the local graveyard, and was a sleep-walker. In some ways, he was a cautious child, but in other ways he was carefree and reckless! Twain liked playing in the cemetery not far from where he lived, and several researchers have wondered about the *affect* playing so frequently in the Hannibal cemetery had on him.

Twain would eventually play with peers of his own age in the cemetery, and their games were imaginative and typical for their ages. Though before this, he had ghost friends in the cemetery that spoke to him and he *spoke* to them. It may be that spirits of the dead — ghosts — were more prevalent in Twain's life than previously known. What was the effect on him, and how did it affect him? One can only wonder and conjecture, though Twain did write books about his experiences with ghosts.

The cemetery where Mark Twain played and had ghost friends.
Courtesy of Deena West Budd.

It is true that Mark Twain was a child of wonder. Wonder's Child is one way of explaining it, for he was always interested in not only what was around the next corner, but also who he would meet there and be speaking with when he got there! Life was full of wonder, despite its occasional mishaps and troubles, and Twain rushed to embrace what was always around the next corner. With the passage of time, what he discovered he wrote about in his numerous books, letters, and publications. His public lectures reflected his findings, too.

The old and mysterious Hannibal Cemetery. *Courtesy of Deena West Budd.*

Another view of Mark Twain's childhood playground...
What paranormal influences did Twain encounter here?
Courtesy of Deena West Budd.

To take this investigation to full-term, let us also consider the possibility that Mark Twain had certain psychic gifts that made him more alert and sensitive to the paranormal world around him. Missouri has long been recognized for its interesting individuals who were blessed with the gifts of prophecy, dream interpretation, and other physic inclinations. There is a joke about such things in the Missouri hill country among residents that it must be something in the water. Still, for the most part, there was a certain reluctance to openly admit to having such abilities in Mark Twain's times, though Twain himself made reference to it in some of his more well-known quotes: *"When I was younger, I could remember it, whether it happened or not."*

Twain's family was reluctant to have open expressions of feelings towards others and rarely showed any in a family setting. In a sense, Twain grew up in this atmosphere without expressing feelings, this environment where personal feelings were best left unsaid in most situations. Yet, Twain did have deep feelings on a wide range of topics, although it would take time for him to feel that he could openly share them.

To read the letters written, and discussions held, by Twain over his life, it is clear that it was not until he met and fell in love with his beloved Livy that he came to openly express feelings with others. In fact, after he married Livy, he came to appreciate and enjoy such open displays of affection. With Livy and their children, he became a devoted, affectionate man and father, and he lavished his love and attention on them. Twain's friends admired his open, natural friendliness and sensitivity. Twain and Livy openly watched over each other with a true love and affection for each other that was the good, honest "stuff" worthy of a serious filmmaker!

To return to the theme that Twain may have possessed some paranormal abilities, the reader need only to look at his relationships with others, his feelings towards the hereafter, and his many discussions and writings on death and dying, ghosts, the spiritual possibility of mistaken identities, and premonitions. Twain was also a prolific letter writer and there is a tremendous amount of interesting material found in his letters. An interesting aspect of Twain was his unique ability to observe accurately, flawlessly, and with an honest approach the emotions and feelings of people, many of whom became the basis for the fictional characters in his books. He had the talent for getting essential details of any given situation he witnessed and writing them down in a lucid manner.

Growing Up

Mark Twain had an inquiring mind, and he was inquisitive. He was not afraid to take risks, and he did not hesitate to pursue an idea for doing something if it appealed to him and proved promising. With his friends, he was liked and looked upon as their leader, though often enough he preferred to be just one of the group and join in. He did not mind the role of being a leader, but only when he felt it necessary or if he decided it was in his best interests and also of those he was to lead! Twain developed a stoic approach to life, and he enjoyed running around with his nighttime friends for whatever adventures they could share together as a gang.

Twain also had a fondness for animals. Although he liked and owned some dogs, he had a great preference for cats and he often had two or three cats at his residences at any given time. He liked the company of cats as pet companions. Some of the names he had for his cats were Sour Mash, Poopsy, Sackcloth, Abner, Bambino, Sin, and Ashes. He made many references to cats, including this one: *"Some people scorn a cat and think it not an essential; but the Clemens tribe are not of these."*

Vintage photo of Twain with one of his many cats. Twain's cats had a fondness for sitting on his lap. There appeared to be a special bond of love between Twain and cats that knew no limits.

Twain's formal education in a school setting was behind him by the time he was fifteen years old, at which time he started working at the *Missouri Courier* doing odd jobs and learning about printing. By 1850, he was ready to move on and did so by going to work for his brother Orion Clemens' newspaper, *Western Union*, as an editorial assistant. It was here that Twain wrote his early sketches such as "The Gallant Fireman," among others.

Orion and Twain got along well together. In addition to being brothers by kin, they were true friends to each other and during these early years helped each other in many ways. In his early writing career, Twain employed pen names to write under; among them are found the names of Josh, Perkins, and Snodgrass. During the often monotonous task of typesetting, he let his creativity and imagination roam wild... and thus was born his early writing of sketches and humorous pieces for publication.

Twain matured fast in the rough river region he grew up in, and soon found himself attracted to women. His ready smile, gentle manners, and charismatic personality made him exceptionally attractive to them as well.

As previously noted, Twain was always interested in dreams, prophecy, and the paranormal. This ongoing interest was further deepened as he observed his mother's interest in such subjects. These interests would later be revealed in his writings. Twain oftentimes wrote about having prophetic dreams and premonitions that became reality.

One of the great tragedies in his life, which scarred him spiritually and mentally, was the unexpected death of his brother Henry in a steamboat disaster. It was a tremendous loss to him — one that he never forgot, nor did he ever fully recover from. Henry Clemens was on-board the steamboat *Pennsylvania* as an employee when the boilers exploded, and Henry happened to be sleeping in a stateroom over the boilers at that time. Scalded and suffering from burns over much of his body, he died painfully. This was a major concluding incident in Twain's youth... one that haunted him always from the year 1858 onwards.

The Next Life Phase

Mark Twain would experience many other traumatic times during his lifetime, and each in turn would leave its separate, independent mark upon him as a man, as an inquisitive individual, and as a writer. His quests would take him around the world, and his writings would reflect what he learned from life, his interaction with people, and what he thought about existence and humans. The older Twain became, the more often there was a sense of dark laughter lurking in his charming voice when he spoke, as if he had learned what life was about in all its intricate, intimate ways, and accepted his role as the writer and speaker chronicling what these ways were! A close examination of his writings, speeches, lectures, and quotes gives the reader further understanding of Mark Twain and his sometimes dark humor. His wit and comments became a secondary trademark to his ongoing popularity as America's favorite writer during his lifetime.

At times, Twain appeared almost tireless in his comings and goings before the world, and the only time he fully stopped was when death stopped him. Mark Twain knew that it was not the name of the dance that was important, but the dance itself, and he lived fully every moment of life's dance without pause. Twain knew intuitively more so than most what the real nature of Shiva's dance of life was about, and this is what follows. *(Author's note: Shiva is an important Hindu god. At once terrible and benevolent, he is never more powerful than when he is dancing.)*

Scenes from a Life Lived

Twain's House at Hannibal, Missouri. *Courtesy of Deena West Budd.*

Mark Twain Memorial at
Hannibal, Missouri.
Courtesy of Deena West Budd.

A riverboat sails late at night along the Mississippi River, near Hannibal, Missouri. *Courtesy of Deena West Budd.*

A late night image of a train near Cardiff Hill at Hannibal, Missouri. *Courtesy of Deena West Budd.*

Lighthouse at Cardiff Hill in Hannibal, Missouri.
Courtesy of Deena West Budd.

Main Street of Hannibal, Missouri, 2010.
Courtesy of Deena West Budd.

Chapter Two:

ADVENTUROUS
YOUNG MAN

"There comes a time in every rightly constructed boy's life when he has a ranging desire to go somewhere and dig for hidden treasure."

~ *The Adventures of Tom Sawyer*, 1876

ark Twain had many adventures, and each one helped form the man that readers came to know through his writings. He came from a Presbyterian family, which had its heritage roots in the state of Virginia; and, he was a practicing Presbyterian during his lifetime.

Twain's life was never boring. He enjoyed living life and confronting its mysteries at every opportunity because, to him, life was a journey of learning, experiences, and coming to terms with what he encountered along the way. Twain enjoyed his time as a steamboat river pilot. His time on the Mississippi River was from 1857 until the outbreak of the American Civil War in 1861.

As an adult, Mark Twain would find people were captivated by him for his charisma and appealing voice. When taken together, it only further added to his legend as his writing career became firmly established. He was in great demand as a speaker during his career. His audiences were captivated, whether he was in private conversation, giving speeches or lectures, or freely mingling in public with his readers. He had a natural wit and sense of humor that served him well in his life.

Vintage 1874 engraving of Mark Twain.

You could say that Mark Twain was blessed with a high degree of mental acumen. Some admirers of Twain often remarked that he had a look of perpetual curiosity in his eyes, and he appeared to be wondering privately, "What if…" However his friends, fellow writers, and readers came to see him as they always knew he was — a man of humorous insights and penetrating comments.

From Samuel Clemens to Mark Twain

There are three versions of how the author acquired the legendary pen name by which the world would come to know him:

• One explanation is that it was a personal choice, a choice based on life experiences, in which he took the name from an elderly mariner's discarded name because Twain remembered the man who had used it.

• The second explanation is that Twain took the name from its usage on Mississippi steamboats in which the depth of the river was watched closely to avoid running aground or other mishaps. The word "twain" was a depth measurement in fathoms whereby a fathom was a measurement of six feet, and "twain" also identified as second, and the word "mark" indicated in river terminology that the precise depth was exactly a fathom mark. This was achieved by the simple yet practical approach of a steamboat deck employee, also known as a leadsman, tossing a line with a weight overboard from the steamboat for measurements and, by doing this safety action, could call out to the steamboat pilot the precise depth results. So, the words "mark twain" meant two fathoms.

• A third explanation, claimed by some researchers, is that the words "mark twain" was a common much-used way to order whiskey in a bar or saloon. The use of the words "mark twain" came to mean a double shot of the bartender's cheapest whiskey being offered.

Vintage photos of Twain
as a young man, taken in
1865, 1867, and 1868,
respectively.

Although there may be still other versions, either discovered or undiscovered, these three have been found by researchers investigating the life and writings of the author, Mark Twain. Readers will find Twain's thoughts on the matter in his remarkable book, *Life on the Mississippi*.

At War

Although he served for a short time in the military forces of the Confederacy, he decided after careful reflection and observation that it was not for him and left. He simply got off his horse and walked away from the winds of war, is one version told, to pursue a more meaningful existence. The following Twain quotes would seem to support this and offer an explanation.

"All war must be just the killing of strangers against whom you feel no personal animosity; strangers whom, in other circumstances, you would help if you found them in trouble, and who would help you if you needed it."

~~~~~

"Man is the only animal that deals in that atrocity of atrocities, War. He is the only one that gathers his brethren about him and goes forth in cold blood and calm pulse to exterminate his kind. He is the only animal that for sordid wages will march out and help to slaughter strangers of his own species who done him no harm and with whom he has no quarrel. And in the intervals between campaigns he washes the blood off his hands and works for 'the universal brotherhood of man' – with his mouth."

Romance and Adventure

There is a wonderful catalog of adventures that Twain partook in, much like in the manner of a medieval quest, but with the end of the quest not ending; rather evolving into another adventure. His time in California also make for colorful reading, and he did romance the ladies as any good-looking young man his age would do. One of his reputed many romances was with the poet Ina Coolbrith (1841–1928) while he was living in Sacramento, California, in 1864. Ina would enter his life again, briefly near the end, when he was a widower.

Twain's various journeys and travels with his brother Orion Clemens appear in different sources, but one of the major reading guides, in addition to Twain's letters and newspaper publication, is most readily accessible in his popular *Roughing It*. People who read *Roughing It* have found this highly entertaining book gives plenty of humor, insights, and details about Twain's adventures as a young man. He could give a description that explained in precise details any given situation and define the attributes of those involved in that situation; and, his comments and humor often masked a deep satire that could be taken in different ways! For instance, in the first two chapters of *Roughing It*, he provides this description of the weapons each member on the stage coach to Carlson Nevada had on their person during this journey:

"I was armed to the teeth with a pitiful little Smith and Wesson's seven shooter, which carried a ball like a homeopathic pill, and it took the whole seven to make a dose for an adult. But I thought it was grand. It appeared to be a dangerous weapon. It only had one fault — you could not hit anything with it... The Secretary had a small-sized Colt revolver strapped around him for protection against the Indians, and to guard against accidents he carried it uncapped. Mr. George Bemis was dismally formidable. George Bemis was our fellow traveler.

"We had never seen him before. He wore in his belt an old original"
Allen" revolver, such as irreverent people called a "pepper box." Simply
drawing the trigger back, cocked and fired the pistol... To aim along the
turning barrel and hit the thing aimed at was a feat which was probably
never done with an "Allen" in the world."

This was Twain's gift: an ability to synthesize while creating colorfully
expressed, penetrating scenes of what was essential, meaningful, and
important. It is not surprising to read a work by Twain and realize
the different themes working together in unison to achieve a given
conclusion. Twain put the reader first in his writings, for he wanted us,
his readers, to understand what he, the author, knew.

Chapter Three

THE FAMILY MAN

"Affection and devotion are qualities that are able to adorn and render beautiful a character that is otherwise unattractive and even repulsive."

~ The Gilded Age, 1873

MARK AND LIVY

hen Mark met his future wife, it was love at first sight. It is reputed that Charles Langdon, a fellow traveler on a Quaker cruise with Twain, showed him a picture of his lovely sister Olivia. Twain said he fell in love at first sight with her, and the romance between Livy and Mark commenced. The two met in 1868. The courtship involved numerous letters and a love affair between the couple through the mail — letters that today show the romantic side of Mark Twain and Livy.

Vintage photo of Twain's beloved wife, Livy Clemens, 1867.

Through Livy, Twain met people in a wide range of professions, including some of the abolitionists who had a strong influence on him, Harriet Beecher Stowe, and William Dean Howells; the latter of whom became a close friend of Twain's and they corresponded frequently with each other over the years.

In February 1870, Livy and Mark were married and, during their happy marriage, had four children. Langdon Clemens (1870–1872) was their only son and he died of illness within nineteen months of their wedding. Suzy (1872–1896), Clara (1874–1902), and Jean (1880–1909) were the beloved daughters of Livy and Mark, who were highly devoted to their children. Both lavished their love and time not only on each other as husband and wife, but also on their daughters. All of the reports and research about Twain's life show that the Clemens couple and their daughters were a happy, active family.

Livy was completely devoted to the well-being of her husband and also served as his editor. Before his writings ever saw a publisher, she saw them first and commented accordingly. This was one of the things that Livy had on her list of things to do, and she prided herself in helping her husband to edit these works.

People who saw them most often agreed that Mark and Livy's marriage was both practical and romantic, and they seemed perfectly paired as a married couple. Accordingly, Mark and Livy lived and enjoyed one of the greatest love stories of all time, and those who personally knew them, including Livy's brother Charles Langdon, said this was the truth about the couple.

When Livy died, it broke Mark's heart. His health started on a downhill journey at her passing and he was dead within six years of her death. Never one for exercise — as this quote from him indicates "*I have never taken any exercise, except sleeping and resting, and I never intend to take any*" — Twain's heavy drinking, heavy smoking, and poor eating habits contributed to his physical demise.

Livy died at Villa di Quarto outside of Florence, Italy, of a heart attack. Mark survived her by six years, dying of a heart attack on April 21, 1910, at Redding, Connecticut. He is buried in his wife's family plot at Elmira, New York.

The letters of Mark and Livy are found in numerous locations, including university collections, private and public collections, and societies dedicated to the Twain legacy. Those interested in pursuing further research into the lives of Mark and Livy together should find much of interest through public library resources and the Internet.

TWAIN AND HIS DAUGHTERS

As a father, Mark Twain adored his children and was protective towards them. Just as the old saying goes that a mother would turn into a wildcat to protect her children if those children were threatened, the same saying applies to a father's love for his children in essentially the same way. Twain would have turned into an instant wildcat had his children been threatened!

Twain also saw to it, along with Livy's guidance and suggestions, that his daughters had access to a meaningful education filled with learning the best of everything life had to offer. It was a matter of letting them approach life on their own terms, savor what life had to offer, and learning what pitfalls and disadvantages also existed. Life was seen as an opportunity to learn, and Twain and Livy made available to their daughters what could be utilized, understood, and enjoyed as each girl progressed and matured into adulthood. Twain also played games with the girls, such as dress-up, charades, mistaken identities, which further whetted the girls' inherited curiosity about appearances and situations. Both Twain and Livy wanted their children to see beyond the façade of everyday life, and they taught them to look for what was unusual, what was the best of a thing or situation, tolerance, compassion, kindness, and discernment.

Vintage photos of Mark Twain's daughters: Susy Clemens, 1885; Jean Clemens, 1898; and Clara Clemens, 1888.

Twain also wanted his daughters to be involved in the creative arts in ways that would interest and entertain them, and to a greater degree, inspire them. If they had a respect for what the arts could offer, they would always have some special bond of attachment with the arts. It should be noted that Twain had a gift for teaching by both direction and indirection. Like most fathers, Twain knew he could not teach experience, but he could teach lessons he had personally learned and personally encountered during his busy life. He could tell stories that made their point through action, confrontation, reflection, and quiet thinking. His stories about his own life and adventures made for entertaining commentaries, and there was always a great amount of humor along with the seriousness.

Livy, a highly educated woman, gave her fair share of input as well, and together, she and her husband made unusual, thoughtful parents! It would have been interesting to witness a night or journey with the Twain family! When the Clemens girls matured and finally stepped gracefully into their own lives, they were more than prepared for whatever life had to offer them.

During the last years of his life as a widower, Twain suffered much mental stress over the behavior of his two daughters Clara and Jean, their personal lives, private goals, actions, and how he could best be of help to them. (Olivia had died on August 18, 1896.) Some critics have suggested that Twain's concern over his two daughters contributed to his death. Photos taken during him in the year prior to his death reflect the face of a weary, old man who, although exhausted and tired, refused to give in to the problems of life. He had the look of a man who had endured, could endure, and would endure until the moment he died! One thing about the character of Mark Twain, he was not a quitter.

As Twain moved into the last year of his life, it was time to embrace the end, as seen in Shiva's dance of life, and come to terms with what followed. When this portion of the dance of life was over, Twain faced and embraced death as he had everything else during his adventurous life — with a smile and a silent question of "What comes next?" For Mark Twain, greeting death was simply another door to open and pass through to other travels, and during the last week of his life it was evident he was ready for a new walkabout wherever it would lead him to a new, continuing version of Shiva's unending dance.

Chapter Four:

TWAIN'S TRAVELS

"There is no other life; life itself is only a vision and a dream for nothing exists but space and you. If there was an all-powerful God, he would have made all good and no bad."
~ "The Mysterious Stranger," c. 1910

*I*n reviewing the travels of Mark Twain, it is important to see how they are reflected not only by the time period, but also in his books. When Twain left for the state of Nevada with his brother Orion Clemens on July 18, 1862, his travels took him to Carson City, Nevada, where he arrived on August 14, 1862. That September he arrived in the Esmeralda mining district near Aurora, Nevada. After sharing a claim, he established timber claims near what is today Tahoe. During this time, he also became involved with heavy speculation in silver and gold mining stocks, and successfully fulfilled the role of secretary for his brother.

From this time on, Twain would undertake many travels, during which he created five travel books. The consensus of literary critics is that these books were well-written and they were all successful. Two books would focus on the United States: *Life on the Mississippi* and *Roughing It*. Twain also wrote three books about his foreign travels: *The Innocents Abroad*, *A Tramp Abroad*, and *Following the Equator*. One of his longer travel books is *Following the Equator*; when it was first published in 1897, it contained 718 pages.

In recent years, a volume of Twain's travels to Hawaii was published. His Hawaii letters, sometimes referred to as *Mark Twain's Letters from Hawaii*, contain twenty letters he wrote as a reporter for the *Sacramento Daily Union* at Sacramento, California. There are twenty-five letters, and they were published in the newspaper from April 16, 1866, through November 16, 1866. These letters, which made for enjoyable reading for those in the United States who followed Twain's reporting, included "At Sea Again," "The Romantic God Lono," "The Great Volcano of Kilauea," and "A Funny Scrap of History." Twain gave America a colorful account of Honolulu and the Hawaiian Islands, known as the Sandwich Islands during his visit there. It would be much later when the Sandwich Islands' name was changed to the Hawaiian Islands, and finally to the name, Hawaii.

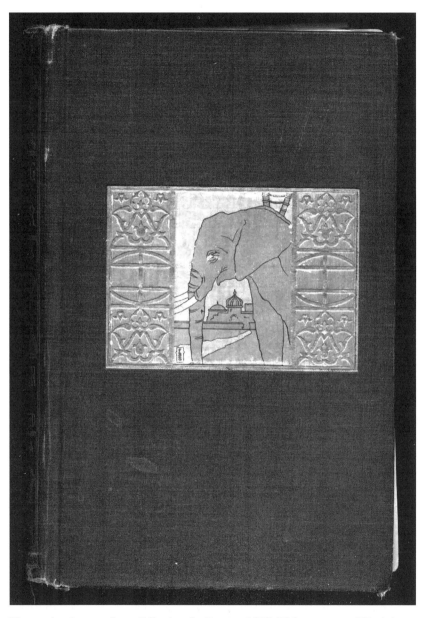

Vintage book cover from *Following the Equator*, 1897. This was one of Twain's longer travel books. When it was first published, it contained 718 pages.

Vintage first edition cover of *The Innocents Abroad*, 1869.

In examining Twain's travel writings, it is best to start with his "Stage-coaching on the Overland," in which he details his stateside journey with his brother Orion. This is followed by his writings, "Salt Lake City," "Carson City," "Silver Mining in Nevada," "Striking It Rich," and the colorful "Virginia City." To actually read these writings is to see, feel, and enjoy what Twain encountered. Other entries in his writings would include his view of "San Francisco," thoughts on "Young Days on the River," "Perplexing Lessons," "Rank and Dignity of Piloting," plus his intriguing entries about "The House Beautiful," "New Orleans," "Hannibal," and "St. Paul and Minneapolis."

Each writing selection has something special to offer the reader with bits and pieces of history found throughout his travels. For instance, on his trip to Germany, he noted that "Frankfort has several distinctions. One being that it is the birthday of the German alphabet; or at least the German word for alphabet — BUCHSTABEN. They say the first movable types were made on birch sticks – BUCHSTABE – hence the name."

As you can readily see, Twain had a gift for travel writing, with many of his writings seeing countless printings, some in different formats and text arrangements. For ease of reference, here is a listing of some of the cities he visited during his travels: Paris, Venice, Rome, Naples, Athens, Constantinople, Odessa, Yalta, Heidelberg, Baden-Baden, Lucerne, Geneva, Ephesus, Damascus, Nazareth, Jerusalem, Bethlehem, Bombay, Allahabad, Benares, Tangier, Alexandria, Sydney, and Melbourne.

Additionally, there are the islands he visited. These would include the Sandwich Islands (now Hawaii), the Fiji Islands, and Ceylon. He discusses the island of Ceylon as being, as he interpreted it, "the epitome of Oriental." The Ceylon writing was originally in Twain's *Following the Equator* (1897), along with his writing about the Fiji Islands. As a point of interest, it should be noted that the writing on the Sandwich Islands originally appeared in book form in *Roughing It* (1872).

People read Twain for different reasons, and certainly his travel writings offer plenty of approaches to understanding him as both a writer and a man. A good example is his observations on "Nazareth,"

"Jerusalem," and "Bethlehem." Like all of his writing, he remains a reflective writer for the most part; as he observes, he reflects. Some of his remarks can startle the reader — this quote written in one of his notebooks in 1898 a prime example: "*There has been only one Christian. They caught him and crucified him–early*" — but it would not be the writing of Mark Twain if it did not do so! Readers will find "A Young American in Europe" and "Dining in Europe," both of which appear in Twain's *A Tramp Abroad* (1880), highly worth their reading time.

Twain wrote about his adventures in "Naples and Vicinity" when the ship he was traveling on was in the harbor of Naples under quarantine. During this time, he had the opportunity to visit Vesuvius and the Blue Grotto. Twain's descriptive powers are found in the following sections: "Then we went to Ischia, but I had already been to that island and tired myself to death 'resting' a couple of days and studying human villainy, with the landlord of the Grande Sentinelle for a model." Further along, Twain observes: "Nero's Baths, the ruins of Baiae, the Temple of Serapis; Cumae, where the Cumaean Sibyl interpreted the oracles, the Lake Agnano with its ancient submerged city still visible far down in its depths — these and a hundred other points of interest we examined with critical imbecility..." Sharp, pungent, and to the point are three ways to explain Twain's ability to isolate and save a given image of what he has witnessed and encountered. He is much like a camera, recording in detail what the camera eye sees, placing the image firmly upon the raw film of remembrance in such a manner that it endures and is available for reviewing again and again. The full text is found in *The Innocents Abroad* (1869).

To fully savor Twain's travel writings, one has to return to its texts currently found in available books. Twain could capture a scene, setting, or situation in sharp, focused prose that left no doubt as to what he had seen. It was most important to Twain that a description be accurate. If he saw something that particularly moved him in some way, he wrote it down as such, sharing his feelings with the readers. For instance, Twain's travels in Heidelberg, Germany, developed into a finely written piece he titled "Heidelberg." In his overall comment on this old German town, he says directly and with much conviction, "I have never enjoyed a view which had such a serene and satisfying charm about it as this one gives." Further along, he writes reflectively upon the scene by saying: "One thinks Heidelberg by day – with its surroundings – is the last possibility of the beautiful; but when he sees Heidelberg by night, a fallen Milky Way, with that glittering railway constellation pinned to the border, he requires time to consider upon the verdict."

Twain's travel writing are important for another reason: they show the great love he had for life and how he lived it fully. They also reveal his astute observations in many different ways. Each observation has its own direction, insight, and approach. Perception was a key element of his writing and he had the ability to make his perception clear.

However, Twain's travel writings were only the beginning. With his journalism background behind him, Twain was able to become one of the world's greatest observers of the moment, capturing its essence in total without error. He did this by writing down precisely what he encountered and witnessed without ruse or false embellishment. This, too, is another important aspect of what gave enduring appeal over the years to his writings.

Twain saw things differently yet the same as any other human, and he sought to reveal those differences and sameness in a uniquely creative manner that gave a distinct feel of universality to his fiction and nonfiction. It was Twain's genius to show this universality in his writings that made him into one of the world's greatest authors.

Chapter Five:

THE DEATH
OF MARK TWAIN

"This is my last trip:
I am on my way home to die."
~ "The Invalid's Story," 1882

*T*he final years of Mark Twain were sad in many ways. Despite his fame, popularity, and world-wide appeal as a writer, the death of his wife took its toll with his health and outlook on life. Some of his most intense and darker writing appeared in his later years, and his correspondence also reflected some of his deep despair and loneliness.

Yet, it must be remembered that there was always an intense, dark side of Mark Twain that developed during his childhood and youth. It was always there. Situations in his later years simply forced it to the surface in more open, visible ways in his wide range of writings, as evidenced by the following quote: "*In my age, as in my youth, night brings me many a deep remorse. I realize that from the cradle up I have been like the rest of the race – never quite sane in the night.*"

This, too, was the genius of Mark Twain, and it added to the overall portrait of the man as an individual and as a writer of some of the most enduring writing to ever be created.

Mark Twain the Man

At the time of his death, Twain was one of the most beloved and most widely read authors in the world. His name was known in homes throughout the United States. *The Adventures of Huckleberry Finn* continues to be read and reread, and reread!

Some questions most often asked about Twain, but seldom answered, include the following answers to those questions:

- He was five-foot-eight-inches tall.
- In his more adventurous days, he was known physically for his charm, good looks, red hair and moustache, and a body frame that was both slender and muscular.

Mark Twain in the last years of his life.

• To many female admirers, he was considered an attractive man and women felt his wife Livy was married to the perfect specimen of manliness.

• He was born color blind.

• He loved old forests and took many walks in them, where he was both an observer and a participant.

For readers interested in what Twain's physical appearance was from birth until death, there is an abundance of vintage photographs available from numerous sources. The public library would be a good first step in locating such material, and a reference librarian should be able to make further suggestions on additional research. There are also websites on the Internet for further research.

Additionally, there is the ongoing interest in Mark Twain's dreams, premonitions, and prophetic visions. Consider this, as a sample: In 1909, Twain foresaw his own death and, in a humorous comment, predicted his death. "I came in with Halley's Comet in 1835. It is coming again next year, and I expect to go out with it. It will be the greatest disappointment in my life if I don't go out with Halley's Comet. The Almighty has said, no doubt: 'Now here are these two unaccountable freaks; they came in together, they must go out together.'" Mark Twain died of a heart attack on April 21, 1910, within a day of Halley's Comet's closest approach to Earth. It is as if the comet arrived to give him a ride home to be with Livy.

Finally, the following facts are often missed or overlooked by those interested in Twain's personal life: Mark Twain had a lifelong interest in parapsychology, predictions, the supernatural, and was an early member of the Society for Psychical Research. Through his friendship and discussions with Nikola Tesla, personal readings, and his travels in India, Twain was aware of the Hindu philosophical system known as Vedanta, Swami Vivekananda writings, India, yoga, and other related material. Read carefully Twain's "My Platonic Sweetheart" and consider the possibilities.

Influences on Mark Twain

Twain had many friends in the literary world, including the Scottish author George MacDonald, Bret Harte, and Artemus Ward. Harte and Twain co-wrote a play together, "Ah Sin," about a Chinese gambler, but it failed after its initial stage run in 1877 and was never revived for performance during the authors' lifetimes.

In regard to Bret Harte and Twain, there are many stories given as to why their friendship ended. One of these stories centered around Harte being vulgarly coarse and rude around Twain's wife, Livy. There was a falling out, and Twain came to see and understand his former friend as an artificial, shoddy writer. In fact, Twain is on record as saying about Harte: "In the early days I liked Bret Harte and so did the others, but by and by I got over it, so also did the others. He was bad, distinctly bad; he had no feeling and he had no conscience." Twain also accused Harte of denying Harte's own Jewish heritage and deriding the Jews. With the passage of time, many critics came to see Bret Harte as writing the same stories over and over again with similar characters and similar plot lines.

Twain became good friends with President Ulysses S. Grant. He felt that Grant had a genuine story to share with readers and encouraged Grant to write about his life and role in the American Civil War and as President of the United States. Twain then published Grant's memoirs to great success.

Twain greatly admired Helen Keller, who overcame her deafness and blindness with the help of her teacher Anne Sullivan, whom Twain also admired. Twain enjoyed conversations and friendship with the journalist Ida M. Tarbell and was friends with educator Booker T. Washington.

However, among Twain's closest friends was the wealthy Henry H. Rogers, who became a poker card player and drinking buddy of Twain's; together they developed a deep friendship; apart, they shared their adventures by way of written letters, which have survived to this day. Twain often took cruises with Rogers on Rogers' luxury steam yacht, *Kanawha*, and he stayed as a guest at the Rogers home. Rogers and his family became a surrogate, loving refuge for Twain following the death of Livy. Both men enjoyed each other's company and the ongoing exchange of personal views on a wide range of subjects. When Henry H. Rogers died on May 20, 1909, it was another shock to Twain's failing health.

Family and Money Woes

Mark Twain was known for helping those down on their luck. He donated money where he thought it would do the most good, oftentimes giving money directly to individuals who had contacted him personally.

Twain overcame going broke and bankrupt on some bad business investments. He toured around the world, wrote about it, and successfully paid off the people he owed money. Twain lived a code of honor that included repayment of loaned money despite the odds, whatever the loss had been. Twain made good on his costs and his losses. Another important aspect of Twain's character as a man was that he never forgot the kindness of strangers. During his life, he practiced kindness where possible and most needed.

Twain had long relished the idea of grandchildren. Four years before he died, he became a friend and letter-writer to twelve schoolgirls ranging in age from ten to sixteen. They became, in a spiritual sense, his grandchildren. It was a way to take the edge off of his illnesses and loneliness in his final years.

These girls became, in the strongest sense, Twain's surrogate granddaughters. Their positive effect on Twain was an energizing one that saw him through to his death. Although it did not take his mind off the death of his beloved Livy, the letter-writing and chaperoned visits from these girls succeeded in sustaining him. Over a period of four years, from 1906 until his death in 1910, this is referred to as Mark Twain's Angelfish Correspondence, as that is what Twain saw these girls as: his "Angelfish."

When the girls would visit him at his home with their chaperons, Twain entertained them and often played billiards with them. They kept him occupied with their positive attitude and qualities of adolescence, making this closing section of Twain's life much like an endless summer with Huckleberry Finn. His grandfatherly approach gave him the opportunity to be a grandfather. One of these girls, Dorothy Quick, went on to become a writer of fifteen published books of poetry and fiction, as well as the personal memoir *Enchantment: A Little Girl's Friendship with Mark Twain*. In it, she writes of her desire to be an author, so Twain develops an author's guild where they are the only two members so they can both teach the other things.

Another look at Mark Twain is revealed in his daughter Susy's book. This book is most likely found under the title of *Papa, An Intimate Biography of Mark Twain* by Susy Clemens. This biography covers the time period when Susy Clemens was thirteen and her father was fifty. Readers will find this an interesting look at a famous author and his daughter. It includes a brief recollection of young Susie meeting a dying Ulysses S. Grant as the former Civil War General and United States President. Susie is also said to have inspired some of the character traits for Joan of Arc in her father's historical novel *Personal Recollections of Joan of Arc*.

Odds and Ends about Mark Twain

In Twain's fiction, one of his numerous, interesting character creations is Father Adolf in *No. 44, The Mysterious Stranger*. It is unknown at this time exactly what inspired Twain to write and name this character, or what part of Twain's dream premonitions sparked the writing about this Father Adolf. A novel with macabre overtones, social commentary, and sexual insights, *No. 44, The Mysterious Stranger* is set in Austria, with the story starting in the winter of the year 1490. In some of Twain's writings there is a sense of prophetic anticipation.

To what degree did Mark Twain have paranormal contact with spirits or ghosts growing up in the Hannibal, Missouri, area remains a mystery, for much of his time was spent in situations that had a strong tinge and touch of the supernatural and his unseen friends in the Hannibal cemetery were part of that growing-up experience. Could Twain see spirits or ghosts? Probably. Could Twain communicate with spirits or ghosts? Probably. Readers are urged to read Twain for the answers.

During the aftermath of World War I, there were many American writers who went to Europe to live and write. This group became known as "The Lost Generation." Ernest Hemingway, F. Scott Fitzgerald and other writers of the 1920s era were reputed to have read one of Mark Twain's most damning commentaries on war with its blind patriotic and deceptive religious fervor. This story, "The War Prayer," published in 1916, included this quote: "*To be a patriot, one had to say, and keep on saying, 'Our country, right or wrong,' and urge on the little war. Have you not perceived that that phrase is an insult to the nation.*"

Mark Twain based his character creations of Tom Sawyer and Huckleberry Finn on combinations of his childhood friends. He is on record as saying this. The character of Tom Sawyer is based on a combination of at least three friends that Twain knew growing up in Hannibal, Missouri.

An interesting observation about Mark Twain was that during his lifetime he was one of the most photographed men alive. Additionally, there were drawings, etchings, sketches, and paintings of him. Today, he remains a favorite subject of artists seeking to capture that special Twain look in an artistic expression.

Mark Twain Lives On

Another aspect of the Twain legend that still endures today is groups of people who gather to read his works and share commentary on his life and times. This includes people performing character role readings from his novels and other writings.

Mark Twain was a man full of life and vigor, and he was always game for the next adventure and whatever encounters it brought to him. It is reputed that Twain still had that mischievous glint of humor in his eyes even during the last week of his life. Whatever awaited Mark Twain in the afterlife, he was more than ready and prepared to meet it sitting around a table of pleasant conversation, cigars, whisky, and heartfelt laughter.

At the end of 2010, the University of California commenced publication of the un-expurged autobiography of Mark Twain. Scheduled as a multi-volume set, these books will contain unpublished material that Twain felt might be too embarrassing to publish at the time he was alive. He suggested a hundred years after his death would be a good time to publish such writings in an uncensored format. The new Autobiography promises to have many surprises, and it will be the autobiography Mark Twain wanted published. It will be interesting to read what Twain has to say now in these forthcoming volumes that he could not say while he was alive.

Mark Twain in the last years of his life.

Chapter Six:

AN AMERICAN MAN
FOR ALL SEASONS

"I am a border ruffian from the State of Missouri. I am a Connecticut Yankee by adoption. In me, you have Missouri morals, Connecticut culture; this gentlemen, is the combination which makes the perfect man."

~ Speech about "Plymouth Rock and the Pilgrims," December 22,1881

ark Twain had the ability to see clearly into the humaneness of a person and he could report what he saw accurately. In whatever genre he was writing, there was also the inquiring spirit of the author investigating, analyzing, and making summations of what he had encountered.

That Twain was popular as a person and as a writer was well-established during his lifetime. He had a knack for saying what was on his mind in such a manner that people remembered it. There were times he said more than he later thought he should have spoken, yet he had the courage and inquisitiveness to say it anyway. This was another attribute of Twain, the man, which attracted people to him. He had the ability to be both a listener and a talker; each role depended upon his circumstances, who he was in the company of, and what he was seeking to know. From all published accounts, his speaking engagements were highly successful and he remained a popular speaker throughout his life.

Twain had numerous friendships with people in the business professions, sciences, and literary world. One of his long enduring friendships was with the engineer and inventor, Nikola Tesla. Twain's fascination with electrical currents, lightning, and related science topics were among his numerous interests until his death. He also saw in the appearance of lightning a prophetic significance or revelation.

This vintage photograph shows Mark Twain and Nikola Tesla in the Tesla Laboratory in 1894. Twain is observing an experiment while Tesla looks on in the background.

It has been said that Twain's correspondence is like reading the ongoing education of a man and how he shared that education with others. Whatever the topic, within the bounds of good taste and personal feelings, Twain did not hesitate to write about to others. Invariably, he made many insightful observations and at times gave satirical analyses of what he had learned or witnessed.

For those interested in the correspondence of Mark Twain, his published collection of letters will prove delightful and entertaining reading. Most of his correspondence had been published in book form and is available at the public library or on the Internet. The reader who delves into these letters will not be disappointed, as there is much to learn about Twain from his personal letters. Here is an excerpt from a Twain letter written to his sister and mother on April 11, 1863: "I have just heard five pistol shots down the street – as such things are in my line, I will go and see about it. The pistol did its work well. One man, A Jackson County Missourian, shot two of my friends (police officers) through the heart. Both died within three minutes. Murderer's name is John Campbell."

Mark Twain's place in American and world literature is assured. He continues to be read a hundred years after his death, and his books continue to sell well. It has been said that in any given minute of time, there is someone somewhere reading the writings of Mark Twain or something that has been written about him.

His enduring fame rests on his unique genius for capturing the essence of a character coupled with a particular moment in time through which that character is defined and exists. As to his published works, literature would be a sadder place without his barbed wit, insight into both female and male attitudes, and sense of humor. Twain wrote in a way that would reveal a character in whole, with absolutely no parts missing or overlooked; to create and write about a fictional character was to present it in a straight-forward manner. His observations towards places, events, and overseas travels also reveal this straight-forward approach.

One of the enchanting things about Twain as an American icon and author is his ability to be reflective towards whatever he comes into contact with and write accordingly. To be a reflective writer is to be a thoughtful writer, one that is willing to consider what is at hand plus what is beyond, and still further, what might be the possibilities found in the beyond. That, too, is another aspect of what has established Mark Twain as a world author popular in all countries.

Mark Twain, Literature Character?

Given the popularity of Twain, the man, it should be no surprise that he has appeared — *as a character* — in other author's writings. One of the best known is the popular "Riverworld" saga written by highly respected science fiction author, Philip Jose Farmer (1918–2009). In Farmer's involved approach, Twain appears as a living character named Samuel Clemens. There were five novels and these novels are considered a landmark series in the genre of science fiction. For readers interested in the "Riverworld" series, here is a listing of the order in which they were published: To *Your Scattered Bodies Go* (1971), *The Fabulous Riverboat* (1971), *The Dark Design* (1977), *The Magic Labyrinth* (1980), and *Gods of Riverworld* (1983). In addition to the novels, there were also short stories in the "Riverworld" series, some written by Farmer and some written by other authors.

Twain has turned up in other writers' stories as well, whether under the name of "Mark Twain" or his birth name "Samuel Clemens":

• Prolific writer Robert J. Randisi featured Twain in one of his western books, known as the "Gunsmith" series. Writing under the pen name of J. R. Roberts, he has Twain appear as a major character in the fast-paced western novel *The Gunsmith 308: Clint Adams, Detective*.

• *Mark Twain Remembers: A Novel* by Thomas Hauser; *Flaming Zeppelins: The Adventures of Ned the Seal* by Joe R. Lansdale; and *Channeling Mark Twain: A Novel* by Carol Muske-Dukes. These novels give different perspectives on the Twain legacy.

• In author Peter Heck's novels, known as the "Mark Twain Mysteries," Twain is presented as a detective solving crimes within a historical context. Interesting reading for their accurate detail, the novels include *Death of the Mississippi*, *A Connecticut Yankee in Criminal Court*, *The Prince and the Prosecutor*, *The Guilty Abroad*, *The Mysterious Strangler*, and *Tom's Lawyer*.

Mark Twain has also turned up as a character in comic books over the years, including Neil Gaiman's "The Sandman," "The Five Fists of Science," "Tales Designed to Thrizzle," "The Unwritten," and "Transformers." It would be interesting to research and locate how many other comic books "Mark Twain" has appeared in as an active character.

For *Star Trek: The Next Generation* (1987–1994) fans, Mark Twain was a major character in the highly popular and enjoyable two-part episode titled "Time's Arrow," which aired in 1992. The character of Twain is based on several aspects of the real-life person, with the viewer getting a balanced look at Twain's inquisitiveness, curiosity, interest in time travel, and sense of humor. Twain's interaction with Data and other members of Star Trek's Enterprise crew make for lively action.

It is amazing to encounter such things, and realize that a writer, well-known personality, or an international leader has suddenly become fodder for the fiction mills across the world. This is said by way of a compliment, for none of these individuals, while living, knew that one day after their death they would be guaranteed to become figures and characters in fiction books and movies.

In addition to Mark Twain, a few examples of real-life public figures appearing in word as characters are self-evident in scope. How many fiction books and movies have the following once-upon-a-time, real, live breathing human beings appeared in: Ernest Hemingway, Joan of Arc,

Wyatt Earp, Nellie Bly, Adolph Hitler, Amelia Earnhardt, Jesus Christ, Geronimo, Agatha Christie, Jesse and Frank James, Eleanor Roosevelt, Nicola Tesla, Sacajawea, Will Rogers, Queen Elizabeth, John F. Kennedy, Sequoyah, Mary Fields, Billy the Kid, Marilyn Monroe, Harriet Tubman, Cochise, and Winston Churchill. Plus there are many others — see what other real life persons you can discover who have made appearances in a fictional setting, whether in book or movie form. It will surprise you! Some individuals take on a larger than life appearance after their death, whether immediately following the death or years hence; legend and actual appearance blend into a mixture that promotes the person being remembered into a kind of cultural icon.

A great, well-acted interpretation of Mark Twain has been through the memorable performances over the years by American actor Hal Holbrook. *Mark Twain Tonight* showcases the essence of Twain in a format that is both educational and enjoyable for a live audience. A versatile actor, Hal Holbrook made many popular movies over the years, including *Midway*, *Magnum Force*, the original horror film *The Fog*, *Pueblo*, *Into the Wild*, for which he was nominated for an Academy Award Oscar, and *Water for Elephants*. A major motion picture of 1944 was *The Adventures of Mark Twain,* starring actor Fredric March as Twain and actress Alexis Smith as Livy. *Mark Twain and Mary Baker Eddy* (2010) is a movie about the last year of Twain's life. The "character" of Twain is played by actor Val Kilmer, who not only gives a stunning performance, but his appearance as Twain is highly accurate from a historical standpoint.

Every culture — every nation — has its own personal heroes, heroines, and villains, and oftentimes these heroes, heroines, and villains fulfill the needs of other nations in ways in which they initially *didn't* occurred in. One example of this is the life and times of actor James Dean. In his twenties when he died in an automobile accident, James Dean is a prime example of a world cultural icon that influenced generations after his death. Without a doubt, Mark Twain is also a world cultural icon and, as such, his life, times, and writings will continue to be rich fodder for movies, fiction novels, and fiction stories.

To the shock of many, a tantalizing book about Twain was published in 2010. Written by Mark Twain scholar, Laura Skandera Trombley, *Mark Twain's Other Woman: The Hidden Story of His Final Years* is the remarkable story of Isabel Van Kleek Lyon (1863–1958), the last personal secretary of Mark Twain. It is suggested she was much more than a secretary, becoming Twain's intimate companion shortly following the death of Twain's wife, Livy. Twain depended upon her entirely, and she worshiped the ground Twain walked upon. There is much in the way of conflicting information concerning some aspects of the relationship, but there was an intimate affair between them. Lyon was employed by Twain from October 3, 1902, to April 15, 1909, at which time he fired her due to the stories his daughters Clara and Jean told him. For over a hundred years since Twain's death, this relationship was passed over by scholars, although information was available, including the writings of Lyon about Twain.

In 2010, when Trombley came out with her book, its publication sent Twain scholars back to researching his unpublished letters and writings to discover what was available about Isabel Van Kleek Lyon. Previously overlooked, Lyon became a point of interest with her involvement with Twain during his final years. It becomes evident during this time that Twain was suffering frequently with physical pain, gout, prostate problems, bouts of impotence, depression over the actions and activities of his two daughters, heart problems, and other aliments. Lyon nursed him through many illnesses. Health problems in the closing year of Twain's life have all but been completely overlooked until now.

For the most part, Mark Twain was not a man who complained of personal pain. In many ways, he took a stoic approach to personal, physical pain. Another look at Mark Twain's closing years is found in the book, *The Untold Story of Mark Twain's Final Years*, by Karen Lystra, published in 2004.

Perhaps, some enterprising writer will one day write about "Mark Twain's last year prior to his death," detailing information from various sources only recently coming to light. This would make for fascinating reading. Over the years, suggestions of such a project for a major motion picture have been circulated. Maybe one of the readers of this book will be the one to write or film that story. Time will tell! Absolutely!

Afterword

MARK TWAIN:
THE FUTURE

*"Never put off till tomorrow what may be done
day after tomorrow just as well."*
~ autographed card appearing on Internet auction site,
February 2002

With the publication of a multi-volume set of Mark Twain's unexpurgated autobiography, it is evident that much new fascination and interest has come to this American Icon in American Literature. Twain's writing has generated new readers with each new generation, and with each generation comes a renewed appreciation for this eclectic and oftentimes enigmatic American writer. People are constantly renewing their reading relationship with Mark Twain's writings and people have come to appreciate his timeless insights and humor. Although he died in 1910, people throughout the world have not stopped reading his books.

If the reader is curious about rare book prices on Mark Twain first edition books, they will be surprised at the prices, and henceforth always on the alert for such esoteric items in garage sales, estate sales, and the proverbial flea market. Search out different avenues, for instance, and see what you discover is the going price for a first edition copy of *The Adventures of Tom Sawyer* or *The Adventures of Huckleberry Finn*. If you really want a surprise, check out the value of a Twain signed copy of *The Celebrated Jumping Frog of Calaveras County*. This, too, is part of the adventure of reading and collecting the writings of Mark Twain — you never know for sure what you will come across or where. Perhaps, one of the readers of this book will write their own book one day about collecting Mark Twain books and the adventures they had in doing it. It is something to consider.

Thank you for reading my book, and I hope you found much enjoyment in it.

Appendix

TWAIN
IN HIS OWN WORDS

"When I find a well-drawn character in fiction or biography, I generally take a warm personal interest in him for the reason that I have known him before – known him on the river."

~ *Life on the Mississippi*, 1883

TWAIN'S NOVELS

*I*n looking at the massive output of Twain's writings, certain works stand out as more read by the public, and these writings will be looked at and examined. As to his most important novels, his story of Huckleberry Finn ranks in the top listing. The following is an accounting of some of Twain's most widely read novels.

Huck Finn and Tom Sawyer

Twain's two most widely read novels are *The Adventures of Huckleberry Finn* and *The Adventures of Tom Sawyer*, both of which are considered American classics and world masterpieces. And, more than one hundred years later, both books remain popular throughout the reading world.

Statues of Tom Sawyer and Huckleberry Finn located at Hannibal, Missouri. *Courtesy of Deena West Budd*.

One of the most photographed tributes to Mark Twain is the statues of Tom Sawyer and Huckleberry Finn at Hannibal, Missouri. The finely sculptured statues have faces that capture the essence of what each boy may have looked like in the novels. These statues appear as if they are ready to speak or move at any moment. Each "boy" seems ready for their next adventure and are simply waiting for the other to come up with one that offers both risk and fun! Should you visit Hannibal, be sure to examine these intriguing statues...perhaps they will whisper something of interest to you when you least expect it.

The Adventures of Tom Sawyer

First published in 1876, this is the story of a young boy who is mischievous, gets his friends into trouble, and then rescuing them from trouble. Yet he has the proverbial good heart. It is captivating to see Tom Sawyer develop a high degree of moral strength as he seriously begins to understand what it truly means to be a leader among his young peers.

(Author's Note: Cardiff Hill at Hannibal, Missouri, was made famous by Tom Sawyer in this book. To visit Hannibal, Missouri, is to discover memorials to what Mark Twain created, which honor both Twain and his character creations. To visit Hannibal at night is to get a feeling that the ghost of Mark Twain may still be around and all you have to do is call out his name and he will join you as you walk. His ghost is reputed to be full of interesting and entertaining stories, and he probably will tell you about the use of the Mississippi River for UFO travels! You never know what he might say. Rumor has, it all depends on the mood Twain is in at the time you encounter him!)

Tom Sawyer is probably about twelve years old. He has two best friends whose names are Huckleberry Finn and Joe Harper. By the end of the book, it is Huckleberry Finn who takes prominence as Tom's friend. Tom also has a half-brother, Sid, Aunt Polly, and a cousin named Mary.

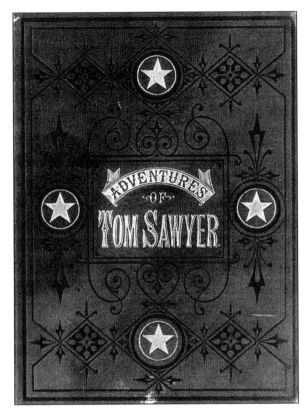

Vintage 1st edition cover of *The Adventures of Tom Sawyer*, 1876.

The characters are well-designed and serve the plot of the story in a complex and entertaining manner. One of the charms of this book is its use of intertwined characters, which occurs again in the Huckleberry Finn novel. Finn is probably around thirteen years old in this novel. He and his friend Tom Sawyer get into many situations together!

An imposing character is Pap Finn, whose death is dealt with in the story. Pap Finn is Huck's highly abusive, drunken father. There is much Pap Finn does to his son that causes Huck sadness and grief.

Joe Harper is the brother of Susie and Faith Harper, and his mother is Sereny Harper. Injun Joe likes to scare the children and strike fear into all of them he encounters in the village. He is a rascal.

Muff Potter is an alcoholic fisherman. He has much affection for children and does many kind deeds for them. Although unfairly accused of murdering Dr. Robinson, it turns out that Injun Joe killed the doctor and convinces Muff Potter that Muff did the murder! It is left to Tom to tell the truth at a possible cost of his own life.

Rebecca Thatcher, called "Becky," is the daughter of Judge Thatcher. She has a love interest in the Tom Sawyer book. The adventures involving Becky and Tom are endearing and full of action. Mary is a cousin of Tom; she is the daughter of Aunt Polly. Amy Lawrence is Tom Sawyer's former love.

Becky's house at Hannibal, Missouri.
Courtesy of Deena West Budd.

Widow Douglas is described as a woman who is forty years old, fair, and smart about things. Huck saves her life after uncovering a plot to disfigure her by Injun Joe. She has a time of it trying to civilize Huck, and Huck runs away only to return on the promise by Tom that Huck can join Tom's gang if Huck will stay with Widow Douglas. Characters in the Tom Sawyer book have connections with characters in the Huckleberry Finn book in some form, with the character of Huckleberry Finn appearing in *The Adventures of Huckleberry Finn*, *The Adventures of Tom Sawyer*, *Tom Sawyer Abroad*, and *Tom Sawyer, Detective*.

An important aspect of both novels, *The Adventures of Tom Sawyer* and *The Adventures of Huckleberry Finn*, is the character Twain referred to as Nigger Jim. The character of Jim, among the numerous white adults in the story, is the only one who could be classified as a true, kind gentleman with a sense of honor about him. Twain took the opportunity to show Jim in this defined manner so the reader could reflect on the society in which the American Negro was forced to live, struggle, and interact with. Aware of the injustices of the world in general, and in the United States, specifically, Twain has Tom Sawyer make it clear that Jim's owner had died and she had freed Jim in her last will and testament. Jim becomes a free man, no longer owned and no longer a slave, and now is permitted the opportunity to make a life for himself.

That Twain was ahead of his time in commenting on and analyzing race-ethnic relations in the United States should come as no surprise once the reader becomes fully acquainted with this remarkable author's writings, as demonstrated in the following quote: "*I have no race prejudices, and I think I have no color prejudices nor creed prejudices. Indeed I know it. I can stand any society. All I care to know is that a man is a human being – that is enough for me; he can't be any worse.*"

As a character creation in fiction, Jim comes across as an authentic person; this is often an observation made by readers and critics alike concerning all of the major characters in both novels featuring Tom Sawyer and Huckleberry Finn. To become authentic for the reader, as if the reader personally knows the character, is what gives enduring life to the novel in which that unique character is created and developed, and sets that novel on the path to immortality as a classic book.

This also explains in part why *The Adventures of Tom Sawyer* and *The Adventures of Huckleberry Finn* are classics. These two novels successfully capture the roots of American society in a given time, place, and situation, which in turn can be reflected upon in comparing what became of the United States after a passage of time, wars, expansion, and economic growth as a nation.

To understand Tom Sawyer and Huckleberry Finn is to understand the United States. Both novels stand on their own merit and can be read separately. To read them in sequence is best. The other novels featuring Tom Sawyer will be of interest to those who find themselves interested in this lively boy as he continues on in search of adventure. *Tom Sawyer Abroad* (1894) has Tom and Huck on a trip to Africa in an unusual hot air balloon. Twain gave the hot air balloon some futuristic attributes. The story is told in the narrative voice of Huckleberry Finn. *Tom Sawyer, Detective* (1896) features Tom and Huck in another adventure as they attempt to solve a mysterious murder. Again, the story is told in the narrative voice of Huckleberry Finn.

Tom Sawyer also appears in three of Twain's unfinished works: *Huck and Tom Among the Indians*, *Schoolhouse Hill*, and *Tom Sawyer's Conspiracy*.

The Adventures of Huckleberry Finn

First published in 1884, there are a variety of characters in this novel, and although some are minor, they each have an intricate role in this American literary masterpiece.

In looking at the characters, we find Mark Twain at his most insightful. The major character is, of course, Huckleberry Finn. Essentially, it should be remembered that Huck is an illegitimate child who runs away from his adopted family and the reasons for him running away is his wish to be completely free of society's expectations. Huck and Tom Sawyer are friends and they remain friends throughout the course of the novel as they travel down the Mississippi River with the slave, Jim.

One of the most delightful aspects found in the character of Tom Sawyer is that he wants life to be led like it is lived and experienced in popular adventure novels. For Tom, there is nothing as exciting as an adventure novel and living life like one! Tom utilizes what he reads as a guide for the most correct and accurate ways to steal, rob, and kidnap — and for creating the perfect band of robbers! Tom encourages main character Huck in many ways and helps him free Jim the slave.

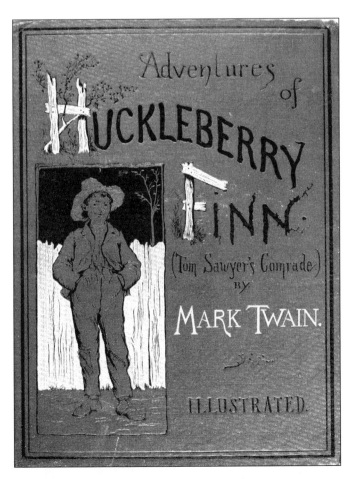

Vintage 1st edition cover of *The Adventures of Huckleberry Finn*, 1884.

Widow Douglas is an intricate Twain creation, one that reflects a feminine perspective on life during her era. Although she does adopt Huck, she cannot civilize him. She is the sister of Miss Watson. The sister makes a determined effort to teach Huck how to spell properly and teach him religion. Miss Watson owns the slave whose name is Jim.

Jim the slave is a pivotal character in this involved story set in the Mississippi River area. He becomes friends with Huck and they form a bond of trust. Two larger-than-life, powerful figures in the story that permeates the book are the Mississippi River and the state of Missouri.

Pap is Huck's drunkard father who is frequently inebriated. Pap kidnaps his son because he wants Huck's money, but Huck successfully escapes. Judge Thatcher is the guardian of Huck's money and is constantly trying to keep Huck free of his father. Pap Finn wants only the money that was given to Huck as Huck's reward. This allows the reader to connect the previous Twain novel about Tom Sawyer's adventures with Huckleberry Finn, and fully understand how Judge Thatcher is trying to protect Huck from his drunken father.

Silas and Sally Phelps are the uncle and aunt of Tom Sawyer. At one point, Jim is being held on their property and Tom and Huck rescue him.

The King is an adult that Huck and Jim take onto their raft. At one point he tells the story he is the brother of Harvey Wilks, and his name is Harvey. His justice comes at the end of the novel when he is tarred and feathered along with the Duke for his various con games, and also for performing badly as an actor in bad plays. The Duke is much younger than the King and he at times pretends to be Peter Wilks' brother William. Peter Wilks is the deceased man who left his estate to his family. The King and the Duke pretend to be his long-lost brothers from England.

The Shepherdson family and the Grangerford family are two feuding families. In one of the fights, Buck Grangerford and some members of his immediate family are killed by the Shepherdsons. Huck and Buck had become good friends, and the death of Buck has a lasting effect on

Huck, who abhors such violent acts. This reflects Mark Twain's feelings on violence and the senselessness of such violent acts, and more subtly, suggests what Mark Twain witnessed during the early days of the American Civil War in which he was in the Confederate military. The personal effect this war had on Twain can be seen and felt through many of his quotes, including this one: "*Before I had a change in another war, the desire to kill people to whom I had not been introduced had passed away.*"

Other characters in the Huckleberry Finn novel include Colonel Sherburn, Judith Loftus, Miss Sophia Grangerford, Harney Shepherdson, Boggs, and Emmeline Grangerford. Mary Jane is one of Peter Wilks' daughters. An interesting character, it is up to Huck to explain to Mary Jane that the King and the Duke are conning her out of money left to her in father's will. Boggs is shot and killed by Colonel Sherburn for being a drunken, loud nuisance.

The novel contains forty-two well-defined and entertaining chapters in which the reader will discover many interesting facts and receive a true feeling for the time and place in which the action unfolds. Twain created his characters based on a composite of individuals he had known or met during his lifetime, which adds to the flavor of the situations these characters finds themselves.

Huck and his adventures capture a young America as it was unfolding as a world nation, and the feeling of the book is excellently revealed in all aspects. That Huckleberry Finn and Tom Sawyer remain enduring American literary creations has long been established and both continue to attract readers worldwide.

There is a permanence and immortality about the character creations found in both novels that has kept the story of Tom Sawyer and Huckleberry Finn alive after more than a century. The books continue to be read and republished worldwide. Mark Twain created these characters to last, and in doing so, created two young boys who were destined to become immortal icons in American and world literature. It was Mark Twain's deep sense of the roots of America that empowered him to write honestly and accurately about the social and political mores of the United States. Both novels can be read on many levels, and there is much subtlety in both. What inspired Twain to write in the way he did so successfully was a combination of factors, starting with his childhood, his youth, his adulthood and his innate desire to capture the United States as it was with underlying visions of what its future could and might hold. Given Twain's sense of humor and perceptiveness, he achieved what he sought to create. Today these two books are considered masterpieces of literature, and they successfully capture an era and a time that speaks to the roots of what America is.

Although Twain would have many more successful books, these two novels have proven to be his most enduring and continuously read. The names of Tom Sawyer and Huckleberry Finn are names known worldwide. The adventures of these two young boys will endure and live on in the hearts and minds of readers as long as there are people to read them.

Other Twain Books

The Gilded Age: A Tale of Today

Published in 1873, its first edition contained 630 pages. Mark Twain co-authored this novel with his friend and fellow writer, Charles Dudley Warner. Although it is carrying two separate storylines, one by each author with the ending chapters worked on by both, the novel's chief charm is its unrelenting satire of Washington, D. C. politics. It can be read today and enjoyed for its timeless humor and biting remarks about politics.

This book successfully satirizes greed, corruption, materialism, graft, and corruption in public life as it was found in the aftermath following the American Civil War. Some critics point out that it gives an insightful look at what was happening socially and culturally in the United States at the time of the book's publication.

For readers, this is Twain at his most satirical when it comes to politics. It is reputed that this novel went through 100 editions from initial publication until the time of Twain's death in 1910. Had the novel been written today, its timeless humor about society and politics would have assured it a solid place on the best-selling book lists! Some researchers and critics alike see the title — *The Gilded Age* — as a commentary on the lost chances and dreams of a United States that could have done better after the American Civil War, but chose not to because of greed and political corruption. Twain seems to support this when he says, "*There is no distinctly native American criminal class except Congress.*"

Readers will be able to see the comparisons from "The Gilded Age" with their own times. As Twain and Warner both agreed and wrote about in their separate plots, the United States became a nation based on greed and political corruption — and it certainly has only gotten worse with high technology. Hence, *The Gilded Age* is as relevant today as it was in 1873.

1601

Published in 1880, because of its subject matter and various decency laws being enforced at the time, the book was mostly seen in small press editions of a limited press run over the decades. When *1601* made its appearance as a long story, or novella, it was rarely out of print. A highly humorous risqué novella, the author remained anonymous from its first publication through its numerous reprints. Not until 1906 did Mark Twain publicly acknowledge he wrote it.

1601 is written as a personal extract from the diary of one of Queen Elizabeth's male servants, her personal cup-bearer. The characters in the story include Queen Elizabeth, her male cup-bearer, Ben Jonson, Francis Beaumont, Sir Walter Raleigh, Duchess of Bilgewater, Lady Helen, Lady Magery Boothy, Lord Bacon, and Lady Alice Dilbery. It should be noted that "Dilbery" is Missouri slang for the word "turd."

Some critics, among them Edward Wagenknecht, consider this unique, imaginative Twain work one of the most pornographic writings in American literature. However, by contemporary standards in modern literature, it is now considered as more of an irreverent story and not obscene. Most critics today see this as classic ribald humor from a master humorist having fun with the English language. *1601* has been compared to Balzac's *Droll Stories*. The original, full title of this Twain humor classic is *Date, 1601*. Conversation, as it was by the Social Fireside, in the Time of the Tudors.

An example from this highly ribald story should give the reader further insight into the manner in which Twain wrote it: "In the heat of ye talk it befell ye one did break wind, yielding an exceeding mightie and distressful stink, whereat all did laugh full sore."

1601 reveals an important attribute of Mark Twain as a writer, which applies to everything he wrote for the reading public: Honesty. Mark Twain wrote from his heart first and his mind second, and if it did not seem true at first light, then he would search for the truth until he found it. When he did find it, wherever he found it, he wrote it down. Twain always seems to write in a manner that explains, examines, and analyzes the situation at hand, whether it is a character, or an action, or a belief, or a combination of all of these things. Sometimes he is more serious in his approach, and in other instances he allows his natural bent towards humor to come through unabated. Such is the case for *1601*, a perfect example of Mark Twain writing from his heart and mind together in sync, with a large, enjoyable dose of humor unleashed upon the reading public. As ribald humor with influences of the tall tale, *1601* is perfectly Twain and Twain is perfectly at ease with it. This too, is the mark of a master storyteller, and reflects why Mark Twain's writings continue to be read long after his death. Twain was a master humorist. This novella is full of ribald humor and has much to laugh at, and about!

For those readers looking for this work, there are various versions of it available. It is oftentimes found in a large, collected edition of Twain's writings or in a collection of his long stories. There is also a free reading version available on the Internet, which can be located on most computer search engines, and some privately printed versions also carry a literary history accompanying *1601*. Much research and writing has been done on this work.

A Connecticut Yankee In King Arthur's Court

Published in 1889, this novel is Mark Twain's great satire with an emphasis of the foibles of human nature, society, and Arthurian fantasy. Considered to be one the first time-travel novels, this book is the story of a man transported back into the time of King Arthur and Camelot. The lead character is a man named Hank Morgan, who comes from the time era of the late 1880s to land in the year 528. During this time, Hank is situated in a high position with King Arthur and becomes his Minister. Knowledgeable in machines and weaponry from his own time, Hank introduces what he knows into the year 528. Hank takes an assistant to help him, a young boy named Clarence. During this time, Hank marries a woman named Sandy and they have a son they name Central.

This is a novel with many intriguing features and it shows how fine of a satirist Twain could be in his fiction writings. He satirizes what Hank brings to the year 528 from the late 1880s. Some of the topics satirized involve the concept of knightly chivalry and the Middle Ages in general. His comments on war and weaponry are sharp, insightful, and to the point.

Twain did not like the writer Sir Walter Scott nor his ideas about war, society, and the role of the so-called goodly knight and, by extension, the role of knighthood. In fact, he blamed Sir Walter Scott for the South getting involved in the bloody American Civil War. In *Life on the Mississippi*, Twain states: "Sir Walter Scott had so large a hand in making the Southern character, as it existed before the war, that he is great measure responsible for the war."

During the American Civil War, the state of Missouri was originally considered a Southern state and an active part of the Confederate States of America. It is reputed to have been represented by the last star on the Confederate flag. Missouri became one of the bloodiest battle states fought over by both sides, with the North eventually winning control of it for the Union. Wilson's Creek in Springfield, Missouri, had one of the hardest fought and bloody battles during the war. Other battle locations between the North and the South in Missouri were at Carthage, Kansas City, and St. Louis, Missouri. Mark Twain's personal encounter with the American Civil War left a mental scar for the remainder of his life and affected his feelings on war, violence, greed, and human abuse.

The novel concludes with a major battle in a cave and by the end of the battle, nearly everybody is dead. Hank then finds himself again in his own era, and he is back in the late 1880s. Hank Morgan was Twain commenting on two eras of time, and through the character of Hank Morgan there is much insight into what humans do in the name of greed, fame, and the ideas promoted by chivalry.

Reading this book today, its observations are fresh and revealing and the reader will find it ranks high among the early fiction writings of time travel. Technically, this novel comes within the genre of science fiction and fantasy. Today, science fiction and fantasy both make active use of the theme of time travel in fiction and movies. For readers interested in Mark Twain's personal thoughts on war, there are many writings and speeches available, including "The Private History of a Campaign That Failed," "What Is Man?," and "The War Prayer."

Pudd'nhead Wilson

Published in 1894, this highly ironic, perceptive novel deals with themes of mistaken identity and race. A close reading of it will allow the reader to readily see what Mark Twain was up to with his characters and the plot they find themselves in. It is an intricate web of problems that befall the characters. Set at the fictional Dawson's Landing located on the banks of the Mississippi River in Missouri, the central character, who the title of the book is named after, is a young lawyer named David Wilson, who believes in the science of law enforcement — including fingerprints in crime scenes. However, because his methods and approaches are considered too new and not in keeping with the locals, he is referred to as "Pudd'nhead" Wilson.

Vintage cover of *Pudd'nhead Wilson* (1894).

People in Dawson's Landing, for the most part, see David Wilson as soft in the head and avoid going to him for legal services. In this novel, Twain created two of his most unusual and complex characters: David Wilson the lawyer and Roxy the slave woman. A close reading of these characters reveal some highly penetrating comments on the social structure of the United States, and as an additional thought, there is seen clearly how some forms of a caste system based on wealth and skin color in the United States do exist. There is the theme of wealth, and how there exists those with money and position, and those without money and position, and the direct influence of where and to whom one is born. It is an oftentimes debated idea that in the United States there is a caste system based on wealth and position. With the proper position at birth or as with the plot of this novel, with the switching of birth of a child and the ensuring mistaken identities of those who are switched, certain advantages are available to the child given position, wealth, and eventual power in adulthood. A film version of this novel was released during 1984 with actor Ken Howard playing the role of lawyer David Wilson.

Twain gives a clear perspective on Missouri and its part in what became known as the antebellum South. By showing that Roxy is 1/16th Negro and Chambers is 1/32 Negro, the emphasis on skin color is readily seen, and how social conventions and social mores focused on such matters, which were, for the most part, readily accepted by both the white and the Negroes of that era.

The plot is solid. The first part of the book centers on Roxy feeling she will be sold to other owners, and consequently, switches the infant son of Tom Driscoll with her own son; her belief, proven true, is that her son will grow up and lead a life of privilege in the upper middle white class. Jumping ahead two decades, a free Roxy returns to confront the Driscoll son who is really her own son and tells him the truth of the switch and how the mistaken identity was possible. She blackmails her real son into supporting her after a bank failure causes her to lose her life savings. The real Driscoll son, having been brought up within a

Negro environment with its corresponding unfairness of social class, is caught up in a world of the have-nots. Other characters in the novel add to the complexity of the plot. In the latter part of the book, Pudd'nhead Wilson enters the mistaken identity confusion and is able to sort out the problems of the babies whose identities were switched at birth. Wilson establishes who is who.

Mark Twain covers different topics in this novel, and he does so very well. He knows the times during which he is writing about, the United States both before and after the American Civil War, and the injustices committed by both the North and the South. As a writer, he is able to utilize his personal memories and the historical aspects of the times and analyze from the perspective of an astute social critic. Even his use of the Italian twins has its subtle points as they are developed as fictional characters in the novel's plot.

Some critics have placed *Pudd'nhead Wilson* among Twain's best novels, saying it shows Twain at his best in the role of social critic utilizing fiction as a logical method to express himself. Twain successfully presented his views on aspects of the United States he found morally wrong, unjust, and unfair. At the same time, he created an entertaining novel that has continued to hold reader attention and endured over the years since its publication.

The theme of switched identities and mistaken identities is seen in full development in this novel. Readers who like this novel will also enjoy reading Twain's *The Prince and the Pauper*. Many readers, having read *Pudd'nhead Wilson*, can readily understand how such themes have progressed throughout American fiction and continue to serve as important supports to plot structure. Twain often interjected autobiographical elements into his fiction, usually knowingly and without apology. Mark Twain loved his country, and he was aware of its strengths and its shortcomings, and the unknown possibilities of its future greatnesses and future failures. He wrote accordingly, and as a result his writings continue to be read over one hundred years since his death.

Joan of Arc

Published in 1896, this otherwise interesting novel lacks the humor of other Mark Twain writings. It originally was published as "Personal Recollections of Joan of Arc" by the Sieur Louis de Conte. Although Twain has stated he considers this the best of all his books, the passage of time, along with reader interest and critical response, has proven this is not the case.

As a point of interest, it is a fact that the actual description of Joan of Arc in the Twain novel was based on Twain's daughter, Suzy Clemens. The description is how Twain remembered his daughter Suzy when she was seventeen years old.

The novel is divided into three distinct parts covering Joan of Arc's life, told from the remembrances of her personal page. Twain spent much time researching the material for his book and it became a personal obsession of his to write the novel about Joan of Arc. As an historical novel, it makes for enjoyable reading and gives a detailed examination of Joan of Arc's life and death.

Joan of Arc is remembered in France for her skills as a warrior and leader of troops, a true spiritual inspiration for the French people, and as an enduring French heroine who was falsely accused and murdered by legal execution. The historical Joan of Arc was captured by Burgundians from the Kingdom of Burgundy and sold to the English. An English ecclesiastical court of law sentenced her to death for Witchcraft and she was burned at the stake as a Witch on May 30, 1431. At the time of her death, Joan of Arc was nineteen years old.

Twain dedicated this novel to his wife, Livy, and it remained among one of his most favorite fiction creations.

The Prince and the Pauper

Published in 1882, this book was Twain's first attempt at historical fiction writing, and it was a success. The book had 418 pages.

The story is set in the year 1547 and involves the consequences of mistaken identity. What all the characters have in common is the ability to persevere. It is the theme of endurance so often found in Twain's fiction: first of all you endure, anything else is secondary. In this novel anything and everything is secondary to enduring what is at hand.

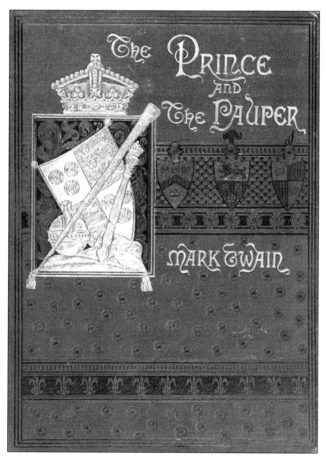

Vintage cover of *The Prince and the Pauper* (1882).

Select a character at random and you will see that each one is caught up in the process of survival, and each much endure to survive. Edward Tudor, the young Prince of Wales, lives an impressive life of royalty, but dreams of the freedom of the city boys such as Tom Canty, who is of the lower class. Living in London, England, Canty dreams of living a life of royalty. King Henry VIII loves his son and wants him to come to the throne. John Canty is an unloving, abusive father who sees his son Tom as a possession to be used as he sees fit. Mother Canty is the mother and Nan and Bet are the daughters.

Father Andrew educates Tom and teaches him things will hold the boy in good stead when he takes the place of Edward and interacts with Edward's family and the royal circle. Miles Hendon is a friend of Edward. Miles is betrayed and displaced in his family heritage by a conniving brother named Hugh. Hugo is the ruffian who is involved in many clandestine situations. Humphrey Marlow helps Tom adapt to his ongoing role as the Prince when Tom replaces Edward. A character named The Hermit is nearly successful in killing Edward when he discovers who the boy really is!

These characters interact and function together in a strong plot that furthers the case of mistaken identity featuring the prince and the pauper. Readers are attracted to Twain's novel for its fast-paced action, and the characters caught up in situations of betrayal and mistaken identity. Each reader forms his or her own opinion on who they favor — the prince or the pauper. Given the story and its time period of 1547, readers have enjoyed this novel on an ongoing basis not only in book form, but also on the silver screen at the movies.

Actor Errol Flynn, twins Billy and Bobby Mauch, and Claude Rains were part of the cast when the movie was released in 1937. A perfect role for Errol Flynn as Miles Hendon, it was a box office success. It has since been seen in other productions on film. The role of Miles Hendon has been played in movies by Guy Williams (1962), Oliver Reed (1977), and Aidan Quinn (2000). A Broadway musical was produced in 2002 with

Rob Evans in the role of Miles Hendon. An interesting contemporary approach was seen in the 2007 film version, *A Modern Twain Story: The Prince and the Pauper*, which starred Vincent Spano in the role of Miles Hendon and twins Cole and Dylan Sprouse.

Clearly, the theme of mistaken, misplaced, confused, or displaced identities and the effects on those involved will continue to surface in contemporary fiction and movies. That Mark Twain is well-remembered by readers for his novel *The Prince and the Pauper* is a testament to his enduring stature as an entertaining author.

The American Claimant

Published in 1892 with 291 pages, twenty-five chapters, and an appendix titled "The weather in this book," this is one of Mark Twain's most unusual books. Over the past one hundred years, this imaginative book, which shows Twain at the height of his creative powers, has been classified as science fiction with fantasy overtones, fantasy, alternative histories with satire overtones, and simply defined to cover all aspects — science fiction. This being the case, then this becomes a cornerstone of American literature dealing with science fiction themes and firmly establishes it in the realm of such writings during the late 1800s.

This book is a comedy. It is also a well-crafted book dealing with role switching and mistaken identities. With such characters as the Earl of Rossmore, Colonel Mulberry Sellers, Mrs. Sellers, Gwendolen, Hawkins, Viscount Berkeley, and Sally, the reader is in for a delightful experience that will keep her or him laughing and curious about what comes next. For those who have not read *The American Claimant*, this is a Mark Twain novel that should not be overlooked!

Many thoughtful critics and researchers have reached the conclusion that had Mark Twain lived, he may have developed his own unique writing approach to the genres of science fiction and horror fiction. In many instances, Twain's dark fantasy was a forerunner to horror fiction.

The Weather in this Book.

Clammat

No weather will be found in this book. This is an attempt to pull a book through without weather. It being the first attempt of the kind in fictitious literature, it may prove a failure, but it seemed worth the while of some dare-devil person to try it, & the author was just in the mood.

Many a reader who wanted to read a tale through was not able to do it because of delays on account of the weather. Nothing breaks up an author's progress like having to stop every few pages to fuss-up the weather. Thus it is plain that persistent intrusions of weather are bad for both reader & author.

Vintage handwriting sample of Mark Twain.

A Double Barreled Detective Story

This is a rough and gritty parody of the English detective story popular during Twain's time. The novel contains rough incidents, humor, and a complex plot in which Sherlock Holmes finds himself in the American West, where times are wild and death is plentiful. Sherlock Holmes becomes involved in solving a murder involving his nephew Fetlock Jones, which takes place in 1880s California.

Note that in the original text title, the word "Barreled" was spelled with two l's. A movie version of the novel was released in 1965. Among the actors in the film were Jeff Siggins, Greta Thyssen, Hurd Hatfield, and Jerome Raphael as "Sherlock Holmes." The movie is said to capture the flavor of the book in its roughness and humor.

Critics are divided over this Twain novel, with some considering it to be one of his more minor books. The first edition is listed as having 179 pages and was published in 1902.

Eve's Diary

This is one of Mark Twain's most popular short novels. It was published in 1906 with 109 pages. It is another of Twain's most widely read books, and has remained in print over the decades. It is a commentary on relationships, love, a sense of wonder at what life has to offer, and how to endure whatever situation or circumstances befall a person in his or her personal life.

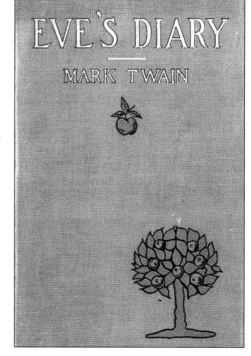

Vintage book cover of Twain's *Eve's Diary* (1906).

This book is the poignant account featuring the Eve of Biblical fame and her relationship with Adam before and after their expulsion from the Garden of Eden. It is part of a collection of writings about Eden, Eve, and Adam that Twain wrote over a period of years.

Told in the format of a diary, Eve explains, comments on, and offers insights. Many critics see this as a love letter to Twain's late wife, Livy, who died prior to the publication of the book. There is also in this cycle of fiction the story of Adam, which appears as Adam's Diary and includes Adam's thoughts on the burial of Eve. In contemporary times, it is not unusual to see both diary entries published in one book so they can be read and enjoyed together.

To read *Eve's Diary* is an enchanting, fulfilling adventure. It is a book that you, the reader, will come back to often. There was always a softer, gentle side to Twain, and this book completely reveals that side to the reading public.

No. 44, The Mysterious Stranger

Originally published in 1916 after Twain's death, it ran 176 pages in length. Most researchers agree that Twain worked on this dark fantasy novel from as early as 1889 until his death in 1910. It is considered among the author's final novels before he died. In 1982, a definitive edition of the novel was published that restored subject matter and material previously deleted in earlier editions.

The story is set in an Austrian village during the Middle Ages. Its main character Theodore is surrounded by a group of interesting individuals, such as Satan (an angle named after his uncle, the fallen Satan), Seppi, Nicolaus, Father Adolf, Marget, Katzenyammer, Katrina, Balthasar Hoffman the magician, Father Peter, Moses Haas, Doangivadam, Martin, Originals, Duplicates, the intriguing character known as the Astrologer, and Mary Florence Fortescue. The plot involves many situations, including burnings, Witch trials, hangings, and deaths.

Twain discusses the concept of self in this novel, and he writes about the walking self and the dream self. He discusses the hypocrisy of organized religion. There is a strength of will in this novel that has been seen all along in Twain's writings, and in *No. 44, The Mysterious Stranger*, the themes of endurance and strength of will are fully realized within the concept of a fantasy approach. An unusual book, it makes for fast-paced reading and the 1982 restored edition comes closer to what Mark Twain intended for his novel before he died. Many critics and researchers cite *No. 44, The Mysterious Stranger* as a continuation and fulfillment of many themes in Twain's writing.

TWAIN'S SHORT FICTION

The short fiction of Mark Twain shows the wide range of Twain's skills with the short story and the tall tale. His knack for pinpointing and revealing the attributes of a given character through situations is clearly defined in this literary genre. Twain had an interest in writing fantasy and what would one day be called science fiction. Some of his fantasy fiction is whimsical and humorous, but some of it is also dark and cautionary in tone. Some of his science fiction could be prophetic. Here are some of his most widely read short stories that cover Twain's wide mastery of the both fields.

The Canvasser's Tale, *A Curious Dream*, and *The Facts Concerning the Recent Carnival of Crime in Connecticut* are often cited in Twain's short fiction as fantasy writing. *A Curious Dream* is one of Twain's more unusual stories and is filled with his trademark humor and observations.

The following is a selected list of stories that reveal Twain's interest in the speculative, paranormal, whimsical, and macabre:

"The Great Dark"

"Mysterious Stranger"

"A Ghost Story"

"Petrified Man"

"No. 44"

"Captain Stormfield's Visit to Heaven"

"Secret History of Eddypuss"

"Which Was It?"

"Which Was the Dream?"

"The Curious Republic of Gondour"

"Earthquake Almanac"

"A Curious Pleasure Excursion"

"My Platonic Sweetheart"

"The Man That Corrupted Hadleyburg"

The above stories will give the reader a more accurate appraisal of what Mark Twain was capable of achieving as a master storyteller, and how he saw and wrote about trends, topics, and his perceptions as to what might unfold in the future. Since the 1950s, a continuing research interest has developed in the above stories and the unpublished manuscripts left behind after Twain's death. Some stories were left unfinished and others were not; taken together, they reveal the versatility of the man as an insightful writer.

For instance, a novella length work, "The Great Dark," may have been intended as a short novel given its word length. In this imaginative story, a ship is making an ocean voyage, but in reality the ship and its crew are inside a drop of water under a microscope being examined by Mr. and Mrs. Edwards. A cast of unusual characters include Alice, Henry, George Bradshaw the carpenter, and the Superintendent of Dreams. This story was written in 1898.

Another story, which was an unfinished novel by Twain, is "Which Was It?" The story covers a period of seventeen years and concerns the evil doings of an aristocrat named George Harrison, who commits murder, steals, and lies. His retribution comes in the form of an ex-slave named Jasper. This story was written in 1902.

Given the changing times and changing literary genre developments, had Twain lived longer he may well have been in the forefront of science fiction and fantasy writers. There are different types in each category of writing. Just as there are tall tales, whimsy, and humor in fantasy, there is also to be found the deepest of horrors and psychological nightmares. Mark Twain anticipated dark fantasy in many ways. Examine the many writers of these genres creating in the era of the 1920s onwards, and it becomes very evident how Mark Twain was ahead of his time and anticipated the advent of such imaginative writings.

"The Man That Corrupted Hadleyburg"

Published in a book collection in 1900 and only four chapters in length, it is one of Twain's most often read long short stories.

The plot of the story concerns a town named Hadleyburg, where the citizens there consider themselves trained to avoid temptation. The townspeople offend a passing stranger who vows he will get revenge by corrupting the town and its people. There is much vintage Twain in this intriguing story, and he does not hesitate to comment on morality, pretense, dishonesty, fraud, and the human condition.

The stranger comes to mean different things to different people. A sack of gold is left with the Reverend Burgess for safe-keeping, and supposedly its contents have a high value of many thousands of dollars. As the plot develops, the townspeople are soon at each other's throats while trying to decipher what might be the message connected to the sack of gold. The town eventually finds the message is a moral statement and the sack of gold is nothing more than a sack containing pieces of lead. The townspeople have learned their lesson and decide to change the name of their town. They rename the town and start anew fully aware that corruption can come about in any setting, and it is up to the individual not to be caught napping when such a situation develops.

Over the passage of decades, "The Man That Corrupted Hadleyburg" has remained among Twain's most read stories for several reasons: Twain's biting wit at analyzing the human condition and Twain's personal feelings against avarice, pretense, fraud, and dishonesty. The story is also a commentary on how greed overtakes reason and honesty without apology, human nature is something that needs personal control if people are to get along with each other in a civilized manner, pride comes before the fall, and one person's fall may be entirely different from that of another person in similar circumstances because pride affects each person differently. "The Man That Corrupted Hadleyburg" is a classic short story and it is classic Mark Twain at his finest. It was released as a movie on DVD in 2004.

Vintage 1st edition cover of *The Man
That Corrupted Hadleyburg* (1990).

"The $30,000 Bequest"

Another popular writing by Mark Twain is this long, comic short story told in eight chapters. Set in a small town named Lakeside in the far western United States, the plot focuses on Saladin and Electra Foster and their encounter with a $30,000-dollar bequest. It is one of Twain's most amusing stories and has an appeal that has kept it alive over the decades. The story was published in a collection titled *The 30,000 Bequest and Other Stories* in 1906 and is available as a movie on DVD.

"The War Prayer"

This is perhaps one of Twain's most darkly satirical stories, and rightly so given his approach to the subject matter. This is a dark, pessimistic analysis of war from Mark Twain's perspective, based upon his personal life of observations. The story is an indictment of war and an indictment of what Twain saw as blind patriotism with its accompanying deceptive religious fervor.

Considered too controversial to be published during his lifetime, the story was not published until 1916, six years after Twain's death. In 2007, a film adaptation was made of "The War Prayer" starring Jeremy Sisto in the role of the Stranger and Tim Sullivan in the role of The Preacher. For those interested in understanding Twain's thoughts on war, "The War Prayer" is the best introduction to know precisely what Twain felt about war and related topics. "The War Prayer" is frequently in print and can be found in different Twain book collections at the public library.

"The Celebrated Jumping Frog of Calaveras County"

Originally published in 1865, this story was later published in a book collection of the same name with other stories in 1867. This was Mark Twain's first success as a writer and brought him national recognition.

The story is about a gambler named Jim Smiley who would bet on anything, and how he came to be betting on a jumping frog. Set in California, the story still retains its originality and charm after being in print for decades after its initial publication. It is the story most found in story collections, and one that gives an insight into how well Mark Twain could handle language and dialog in his fiction.

"Captain Stormfield's Visit to Heaven"

Published in 1909, this story is considered by critics to be Twain's last published story prior to his death. It is the story of Captain Elias Stormfield and his cosmic journey to heaven including his accidental misplacement. This witty tale shows Twain's skills as a social moralist and satirist. Twain is successfully able to show in no uncertain terms that the prevalent conception of heaven is both silly and ludicrous; he does not hesitate to reveal the absurdity and inappropriateness of beliefs in such a misconstrued heaven.

One of the important ideas Twain details is that the conventional image of angels is an illusion. As a point of interest, it is noted that Mark Twain spent his last times at Redding, Connecticut, in a residence he named "Stormfield." A description of Twain's residence can be found in his *Memories of Mark Twain* in Bermuda. Twain said he was fully at peace and happy in his home despite his loneliness without Livy being with him. The house burned down on July 25, 1923. For researchers and Mark Twain scholars, this last residence provides many meaningful clues to the end of Twain's life. He did entertain, and he did write, and he did enjoy seeing his many old friends, and new friends, too. Contrary to popular myth surrounding Mark Twain's final years without Livy, Mark Twain was not a misanthrope, far from it.

~~~~~

Mark Twain created many enduring stories. Here are some of his most popular ones that are considered traditional fiction. Some stories will be more known to the reader than others. Most are found in Mark Twain anthologies of his short fiction.

"The Trials of Simon
    Erickson"
"The Story of the Bad Little
    Boy"
"A Medieval Romance"
"Among the Fenians"
"Concerning
    Chambermaids"
"Among the Spirits"
"Political Economy"
"My Watch"
"Science vs. Luck"
"A Dog's Tale"
"The Story of the Good Little
    Boy"
"The Story of the Old Ram"
"Tom Quartz"
"Buck Fanshaw's Funeral"
"The Trials of Simon
    Erickson"
"How I Edited an
    Agricultural Paper"
"The Facts in the Great Beef
    Contract"
"A Trial"

"Journalism in Tennessee"
"A Day at Niagara"
"Cannibalism in the Cars"
"Legend of the Capitoline
    Venus"
"A Fable"
"A Horse's Tale"
"A Burning Brand"
"The Professor's Yarn"
"The Stolen White Elephant"
"The Man Who Put Up At
    Gadsby's"
"What Stumped the Bluejays"
"Two Little Tales"
"The Death Disk"
"The Danger of Lying in
    Bed"
"The Californian's Tale"
"A Telephonic Conversation"
"Amended Obituaries"
"General Washington's
    Negro Body-Servant"
"Advice to Little Girls"
"A Deception"
"Portrait of King William III"

"Wit Inspirations of the
    'Two-Year-Olds'"

"Does the Race of Man Love
    a Lord?"

"The Belated Russian
    Passport"

"The Five Boons of Life"

"The First Writing Machines"

"A Burlesque Biography"

"Edward Mills and George
    Benton: A Tale"

"A Humane Word from
    Satan"

Letters from the Earth is a book containing some of Mark Twain's most controversial short stories. The book was edited for publication in 1939 by Bernard De Voto, but was not published until 1962.

There is also a series of short stories dealing with God and Christianity. The title story, "Letters from the Earth," contains eleven letters. These eleven letters are written by the archangel Satan to archangels Gabriel and Michael. These stunning letters allow Twain to state his uncensored perspectives on God and the religion of Christianity. Other stories in the collection include "From an English Notebook," "The Gorky Incident," "A Cat-Tale," and "The Damned Human Race."

Overall, these stories reveal Twain at his iconoclastic best, and show a man honestly challenging the way traditions influence humans. That Twain speaks his mind and shares his feelings is evident in this book, and it explains why his last surviving daughter sought for over fifty years to keep these stories suppressed and unavailable to the public.

TWAIN'S NON-FICTION

Mark Twain was also a prolific nonfiction writer, and he did numerous writings in nonfiction. Some of these many fine writings are being read today with much interest for the insights offered into the character of Twain and the times in which he lived and wrote.

Roughing It

Classified as travel literature, it is a long work containing 607 pages. Written during 1870–1871 and published in 1872, it covers the years of 1861 to 1867 in Twain's life.

Although this fine book is classified in the genre of travel literature, it is a semi-autobiographical account and also serves as Twain's personal memoir of his adventures as a young man. After a brief stint as a Confederate cavalry militiaman/soldier during the opening of the American Civil War, Twain realizes the war is about greed, territory acquisition, control of regional economies, and two distinctly different lifestyles, and is not a true slavery issue. Mark Twain was an abolitionist, and he rejected the violence of the war and walked away from a war that was based on lies. He quickly joined his brother Orion Clemens, who had been appointed as Secretary of Nevada territory for the governor of Nevada, and together they went to the American Wild West of the 1860s.

The stagecoach took the brothers where they wanted to go. Twain's adventures include his involvements in real estate speculation, a visit to Salt Lake City, Nevada, his prospecting for gold and silver, and a trip to Hawaii.

An excellent, well-made movie was made of these adventures titled *Roughing It* in 2002 featuring actor James Garner in the role of an older Twain reflecting on his adventures as a young man. The movie was well-received and is available on DVD. For those wishing to see the story of Twain's early adventures and the observations he made from them, this is an ideal movie to watch, learn from, and enjoy. In addition to Garner, the movie has a cast of well-known actors and actresses including Eric Roberts, Jill Eikenberry as Livy, Robin Dunne as the young Twain, Adam Arkin, and Ned Beatty.

Vintage first edition cover of *Roughing It* (1872).

Many readers and critics alike have said this book reveals the foundations of the evolving humor and social analyses of Mark Twain, and illustrate the insightful manner in which he observes situations and people. Twain relied on his life experiences and encounters in his writing, and his many well-known fictional characters are based on composites of real-life people. An example of this is Annie Laurie Hawkins, who became the fictional character of Becky Thatcher in Twain's novels. Twain had a keen ability for understanding the character of another person and he wrote accordingly. This is another reason for his books having an enduring appeal.

For a writer, characterization is of prime importance, followed by plot, action, and theme. In Mark Twain's case, he was able to master each, place each into a complete form, and write entertainingly. In literature, there are many writers who achieve greatness with one or two important novels; others are popular during their lifetime, but are forgotten years after their deaths.

Vintage 1st edition cover of *Life on the Mississippi* (1883).

For Mark Twain, he wrote many important books, and his enduring writings have remained classics that continue to be read over one hundred years after his death on April 21, 1910. In fact, it has been said, there are more copies of Mark Twain's writings still being republished than that of many contemporary writers. People are the final judge of what continues to be read, and they have chosen Twain to read and re-read as an author of living literature. Each new generation discovers something that appeals to them in the writings of Mark Twain and they seek out his writings wherever they are available.

Life on the Mississippi

Published in 1883, the book contained sixty chapters, 624 pages, and was illustrated. This is Mark Twain's personal memoir of his days on the Mississippi River as a steamboat pilot. It is a true memoir from Twain's perspective of the steamboat era on the Mississippi River before and after the American Civil War. The first part of the book reveals Twain as the trainee learning to become a riverboat pilot under his mentor, Horace Bixby, and how Twain came by his literary name. Twain was actively involved with steamboat employment from 1857–1861, receiving his steamboat pilot license on April 9, 1859. Many stories are given as they affected the author's life. In May 1861, Twain's career ends because of the American Civil War.

The remainder of the book is a very frank, insightful, and oftentimes humorous appraisal of life in the United States after the American Civil War, with Twain reflecting on the differences between the North and the South. His observations on greed, among other topics, make for highly interesting reading. Chapter 60, "Speculations and Conclusions," concludes the book. Many researchers have suggested that if the reader wants to know what made Twain the man he was and how his fictional backgrounds took form, this is the book to read first. Critics and readers alike agree that *Life on the Mississippi* is a masterpiece.

The Innocents Abroad

This non-fiction travel book was published in 1869. Research has found it to be one of the most popular, best-selling travel literature books ever written, and also one of Mark Twain's most best-selling books. Its 685 pages are full of Mark Twain's unique, perceptive comments.

At the time of publication, this book was also known as *The Innocents Abroad* or *The New Pilgrims' Progress*. Throughout Twain's life, he referred to this book as his great pleasure excursion.

Vintage 1st edition cover of *The Innocents Abroad* (1869).

The trip commences on the chartered ship, the *USS Quaker City*. Among the stops are Europe and what was considered the Holy Land. The trip takes place in 1867 with other American travels. The coast of the Mediterranean Sea is also visited during the travels. There is a train trip from Marseilles, France, to Paris, France, for the 1867 Paris Exhibition. There is also a side trip through the Black Sea to Odessa to the Holy Land.

Throughout these travels, Mark Twain is in top form with his comments, observations, insights, and recording of what he sees along the way. Read today, this book still contains its biting humor and sense of place and time. For those interested in Mark Twain as a travel literature author, this is a fine book to read and reflect on. Twain is bluntly honest in his observations on places, scenes, and the people he encounters, and what he says makes for humorous, insightful reading.

A Tramp Abroad

Published in 1880, this non-fiction book, classified as travel literature at 649 pages, examines the journey Twain took with his fictional friend named Harris, who is based on Twain's real-life friend Joseph Twichell. These humorous travels place Twain and his friend in southern and central Europe, and they find themselves traveling to many unusual locations, including the Alps, Germany, and Italy. The travels are seen through the eyes of an American tourist, Mark Twain, and reflect his observations and insights. This book is considered a sequel to *The Innocents Abroad*.

Vintage cover of *A Tramp Abroad* (1880).

How to Tell a Story and Other Essays

Published in 1897, this collection of essays covers a variety of topics. The titles give clues to what Twain wished to share in print with his readers, and each essay is a special gem of wisdom and insightful observation as only Twain could have written it.

The essays are short, concise, and to the point, which is how Twain intended them to be. The titles of the essays are as follows: "How to Tell a Story," "The Wounded Soldier," "The Golden Arm," "Mental Telegraphy Again," "The Invalid's Story," "Fenimore Cooper's Literary Offenses," and "Traveling With a Reformer."

Reading a Mark Twain essay is like sitting down in a comfortable chair next to a favorite older uncle, who, once he has your attention and interest, proceeds to spin a story about a subject that becomes progressively more interesting and involved with the passage of time... until suddenly you realize your favorite older uncle is saying nothing more, being quiet, and waiting for it all to sink in so you can make your own comment. This is a good way to look at how Twain wrote an essay. Yet, this was also a gift of Twain as a writer and it holds true of everything he wrote for publication. Twain never sought to bore his readers; he sought only to entertain them with some thoughtful insights, observations, comments, and a good story that would be remembered long after the telling was completed.

Christian Science

Published in 1907, this is a caustic nonfiction work, full of wit, humorous observations, and satire on the religion known as Christian Science. This religion was founded and developed by Mary Baker Eddy.

Twain started writing his book in 1898, and it was completed and published in 1907. In addition to an in depth investigation into the laws, regulations, and beliefs of Christian Science, Twain also commented on Mary Baker Eddy's religious fantasies. In fact, he went into great detail discussing the founding of the religion and its founder's personal background. Critics believe that Twain's lifelong dislike of organized religion because of its innate use of political and social control added to his personal need to write about the Christian Science. At an earlier time, he had written about the Mormon religion in a caustic manner.

During his lifetime, Twain often made analytical comments about religion and organized religions. He felt that this religion known as Christian Science had a chance to become a major political influence in the United States, but he regarded organized religion with a large money base at its disposal as a major threat to the spiritual integrity of the human race. Readers should keep in mind that Mark Twain believed in the integrity of the human spirit, and when he perceived a threat to it — from whatever source or approach — he reacted accordingly and wrote about that threat in such a way that his readers would feel, understand, and confront what he had discovered about such a situation and come to terms with it. Christian Science is an example of Twain doing precisely that because Twain hated pretense and deception in life, whatever guise it appeared in, and he took an active stand against it.

Readers should also remember Mark Twain's accumulated life experiences and the times he lived through. Twain had a social conscience that frequently got him into trouble, but overall, helped him to undertake and write some of the greatest literature of all time. Whether he was writing fiction or nonfiction, Twain wrote about what he knew, what he saw, what his intuition told him, and his personal concept of integrity and honor, which did not allow for any pretense or deception.

TWAIN SPEECHES, LECTURES, & CORRESPONDENCE

Mark Twain was a charismatic individual, and he generally had a large crowd attending his numerous speeches and lectures, for he had an established reputation as a humorist and as an individual having the ability to make insightful remarks with his satire. Mark Twain was well-known for his comments and quotes. He was also a prolific letter writer. As a letter writer, his insights and comments are as interesting to read and reflect upon as his fiction and nonfiction. There is little that he did not comment on! A good search of various book stores, new and used, the public library, and various booksellers on the Internet will locate these volumes of letters Twain wrote over his lifetime.

A research topic that may appeal to many is one concerning the subject matter of Mark Twain's correspondence. It is a gold mine waiting to be searched for nuggets of ore. One such topic is Twain's remarks and intense comments on religion.

"Religion consists in a set of things which the average man thinks he believes and wishes he was certain of."

"Our Bible reveals to us the character of our god within minutes and remorseless exactness. It is perhaps the most damnatory biography that exists in print anywhere. It makes Nero an angel of light and leading by contrast."

"By this time you will have noticed that the human being's heaven has been thought out and constructed upon an absolutely definite plan; and that this plan is, that it shall contain, in labored detail, each and every imaginable thing that is repulsive to a man, and not a single thing he likes!"

"It ain't the parts of the Bible that I can't understand that bother me, it is the parts that I do understand."

~~~~~

However, select *any* topic and there is a good chance that Twain wrote and spoke about it at some point in his lifetime. When reading the letters of Mark Twain, one thing that certainly makes itself very clear to the reader is that the man did not mince words and spoke his mind.

In Twain's speeches and lectures, he maintains his straight-forward approach and in a humorous manner. Many gems of wisdom were spoken in Twain's speeches and lectures, whether in the United States, overseas, or elsewhere. To borrow an old adage, Twain knew how to express a well-turned phrase, and to he could say it with a sense of verve and style that enchanted his listener.

Readers will find these following quotes contained within Twain's writings. They should provide further insight into the nature, personality, and genius of Mark Twain.

"Our Civil War was a blot on our history, but not as great a blot as the buying and selling of Negro souls."

"When he got well, he was a little discouraged, but he resolved to keep on trying anyhow."

"In the first place God made idiots. This was for practice. Then he made School Boards."

"Sanity and happiness are an impossible combination."

for replying to seekers after "opinions"
(otherwise Compliments)
Dr Sir or Madam :
     Experience has not
taught me very much; still it
has taught me that it is not
wise to criticise a piece
of literature, except to an
enemy of the person
who wrote it ; then, ~~that~~
~~even~~ if you praise it,
that enemy admires you
for your honest man-
liness, + if you dispraise
it he admires you for
your sound judgment.
               Yrs truly
                 SLC

Vintage handwriting sample of Mark Twain.

Always acknowledge a fault
frankly. This will throw those
in authority off their guard
& give you opportunity to com-
mit more.

Yours truly,
Saml L. Clemens
Mark Twain

July 3 '77.

"We have reason to believe that there will be laboring men in heaven; and also a number of Negroes, and Esquimaux, and Tierra del Fuegans, and Arabs, and a few Indians, and possibly even some Spaniards and Portuguese. All things are possible with God."

"I became invisible and joined them."

"I had been having considerable trouble with my wings."

"Happiness ain't a thing in itself – it's only a contrast with something that ain't pleasant."

"'In God We Trust.' I don't believe it would sound any better if it were true."

"There is no other life; life itself is only a vision and a dream for nothing exists but space and you. If there was an all-powerful God, he would have made all good, and no bad."

"Let us so live that when we come to die even the undertaker will be sorry."

"One of the most striking differences between a cat and a lie is that a cat has only nine lives."

"Don't part with your illusions. When they are gone you may still exist, but you have ceased to live."

"Clothes make the man. Naked people have little or no influence on society."

"An inglorious peace is better than a dishonorable war."

"When a man loves cats, I am his friend and comrade, without further introduction."

"There is only one India! It is the only country that has a monopoly of grand and imposing specialties."

"My memory was never loaded with anything but blank cartridges."

"It is easier to stay out than get out."

"Man is the only animal that blushes. Or needs to."

"In my age, as in my youth, night brings me many a deep remorse. I realize that from the cradle up I have been like the rest of the race — never quite sane in the night."

"Pity is for the living, envy is for the dead."

"It is better to deserve honors and not have them than to have them and not to deserve them."

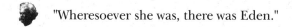

"Wheresoever she was, there was Eden."

"I awoke, and found myself lying with my head out of the bed and 'sagging' downward considerably – a position favorable to dreaming dreams with morals in them, but not poetry."

"Let us be thankful for the fools. But for them the rest of us could not succeed."

"A man cannot be comfortable without his own approval."

"It is hard to forget repulsive things."

"We journey thither tomorrow to see the celebrated ruins."

"If you tell the truth you don't have to remember anything."

"The best way to cheer yourself is to try to cheer someone else up."

"It is better to keep your mouth closed and let people think you are a fool than to open it and remove all doubt."

"I was gratified to be able to answer promptly. I said 'I don't know.'"

"Everyone is a moon and has a dark side which he never shows to anybody."

"Courage is resistance to fear, mastery of fear – not absence of fear."

"When angry, count four; when very angry, swear."

"When we remember that we are all mad, the mysteries disappear and life stands explained."

BIBLIOGRAPHY

ark Twain's writings continue to be published and republished. For the reader's consideration, here are some of those writings with publication dates. These publications can be found at many libraries and through the various computer online search engines. For those interested in researching and reading the vast biographical and critical resources available on Mark Twain, they, too, are available at many libraries on online computer searches.

The Celebrated Jumping Frog of Calaveras County (1867)

The Innocents Abroad (1869)

Roughing It (1872)

The Gilded Age (1873)

Sketches Old and New (1875)

Old Times on the Mississippi (1876)

The Adventures of Tom Sawyer (1876)

A Murder, a Mystery, and a Marriage (1876)

Punch, Brothers, Punch and other Sketches (1878)

A Tramp Abroad (1880)

1601 (1880)

The Prince and the Pauper (1882)

Life on the Mississippi (1883)

The Adventures of Huckleberry Finn (1884)

A Connecticut Yankee in King Arthur's Court (1889)

The American Claimant (1892)

Merry Tales (1892)

Those Extraordinary Twins (1892)

The 1,000,000 Bank Note and Other New Stories (1893)

Tom Sawyer Abroad (1894)

The Tragedy of Pudd'nhead Wilson (1894)

Tom Sawyer, Detective (1896)

Personal Recollections of Joan of Arc (1896)

How to Tell a Story and Other Essays (1897)

Following the Equator (1897)

Is He Dead?: A Comedy in Three Acts (1898)

The Man That Corrupted Hadleyburg (1900)

The $30,000 Bequest and Other Stories (1906)

Eve's Diary (1906)

A Horse's Tale (1907)

Captain Stormfield's Visit to Heaven (1909)

Letters from the Earth (1909)

My Platonic Sweetheart (1912)

No. 44, The Mysterious Stranger (1916)

The Writings of Mark Twain edited by Albert Bigelow Paine in 37 vols. (1922)

Mark Twain's Autobiography (1924)

Mark Twain's Notebook (1935)

Mark Twain's Autobiography (2010), unexpurgated edition, multi-volumes.

Collected Letters of Mark Twain (five volumes, ongoing series as of 2011)

ADDITIONAL SUGGESTED READINGS

Anderson, Frederick & other editors. *Mark Twain's Notebooks & Journals*, 3 volumes, Berkeley, California: 1975-1976-1977-1978-1979.

Baetzold, Howard G., and Joseph B. McCullough, editors. *The Bible According to Mark Twain*. New York, New York: 1995

Burns, Ken, Geoffrey C. Ward, and Dayton Duncan. *Mark Twain*. New York, New York: Knopf, 2001.

Clemens, Clara. *My Father, Mark Twain*. New York, New York: 1931.

Miller, Stuart. *Essays and Sketches of Mark Twain*. New York, New York: Barnes & Noble, 1995.

Neider, Charles, editor. *The Complete Humorous Sketches and Tales of Mark Twain*. Garden City, New Jersey: Doubleday & Company, 1961.

Neider, Charles, editor. *The Travels of Mark Twain*. New York, New York: Coward-McCann. Inc., 1961.

Twain, Mark. *Mark Twain Speeches*. New York, New York: Harper & Brothers, 1923.

Willis, Resa. Mark and Livy. *The Love Story of Mark Twain and the Woman Who Almost Tamed Him*. New York, New York: Atheneum, 1992.

INTERNET RESOURCES

http://uufe-dialogue.blogspot.com/2009/08/mark-twain-and-hinduism.html

http://www.neuronet.pitt.edu/~bogdan/tesla/ontwain.html

http://Classiclit.about.com/cs/profileswriters/p/aa_marktwain.htm

www.marktwainbooks.org

www.gradesaver.com/author/mark-twain

www.thisismarktwain.com

http://cmgww.com/historic/twain/index.php

www.marktwain.cave.com

www.readprint.com/author-83

www.examiner.com/mark-twain-in-national/marktwain-on

www.mtwain.com/l_biography.html

INDEX